Praise for *Doing What Must Be Done*

"My wife Ramona and I dropped everything the minute we got a preliminary copy of Chad's book. We read it together. There were so many moments when we had to stop and catch our breath before continuing. Chad's words inspired us to be better people, more committed to every facet of life, and more grateful for the simple things. We finished the book and spontaneously held each other and wept. We felt so alive!"

- Dave Blanchard, President and CEO of TheOgmandinoGroup.com

"Following this story over the last 10 years has amazed us. Looking back, no one would believe such a story existed. Now, we have living proof! The world needs news like this. There is so much for us all to accomplish, even during difficult times, if we will be persistent in accomplishing what the world would say is unachievable! Chad Hymas has demonstrated that life truly holds NO boundaries."

- NBC

wise
Smart
Connecting
Rituals
for
Peace

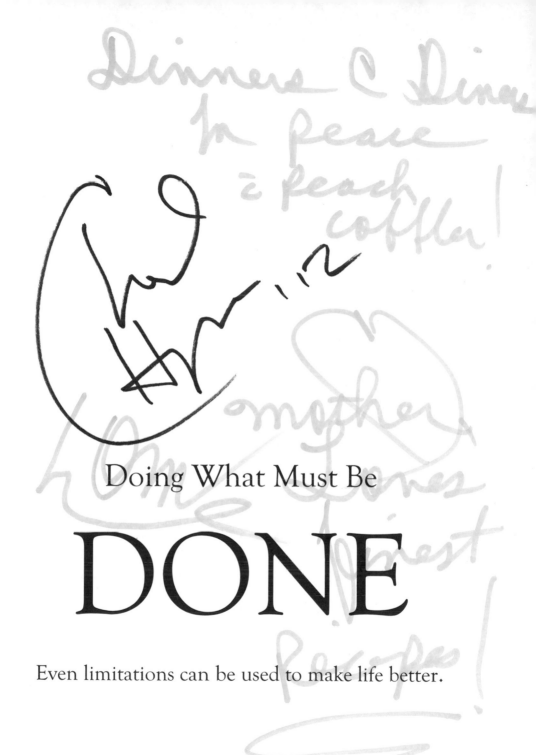

Doing What Must Be

DONE

Even limitations can be used to make life better.

Chad Hymas

Doing What Must Be

DONE

Even limitations can be used to make life better.

Chad Hymas

Chad Hymas Communications

Doing What Must Be DOne -
Even limitations can be used to make life better.

Creative Editor, Tom Cantrell
Tom@TomCantrell.com

Editor: Rebecca Hayes
www.rebeccahayes.us

Chad Hymas Communications
ChadHymas.com
Chad@ChadHymas.com
877-266-5242

ISBN-13: 978-0-9848615-0-7

Library of Congress Control Number 2011961094

This book is dedicated to you, the reader, in hopes that you will find the same achievements and joy that I have found through life's turmoil and challenges.
Doing What Must Be Done is a call to action for YOU!
And in the end, as your journey unfolds, you too will understand what your passion is
and reach your full potential.

– Chad Hymas

In Gratitude

Much work from many individuals has brought this book to the
shelves and into your hands. I can't thank you all enough.
You know who you are.

And to the reader… Yes YOU, THANK YOU
for allowing me to share with you.

Shondell, where would I be without your continuous support and
unwavering faith? I love you and will forever
be grateful for all you've given me.

Table of Contents

Special Note to Readers: Some of the images you see included in this book will appear badly blurred. These images were extracted from a low-resolution video, but were deemed important to the story.

I long to accomplish a great and noble task,
but it is my chief duty to accomplish small tasks,
as if they were great and noble.

~Helen Keller

About the Author

Chad Hymas is a much sought-after business consultant, speaker, author, and coach. As CEO of Chad Hymas Communications, he travels the world, helping organizations and individuals to have a purpose driven approach to leadership and a life that will lead them to prosperity and happiness.

On April 3, 2001, Chad's life changed instantaneously when a falling one-ton bale of hay broke his neck. He was pronounced a quadriplegic, paralyzed from the chest down with limited function of his arms and hands.

Chad is one of four world-class authors renowned in the book "Speaking of Success." He is a World Record wheelchair athlete and set a new world record by wheeling his chair from Salt Lake City to Las Vegas (513 miles) in July 2003. He has been named "One of the Ten Most Inspirational People In The World" by the Wall Street Journal.

Chad is among the youngest ever to receive the CSP (Certified Speaking Professional) award, and is the youngest ever to be inducted into the prestigious Speaker Hall of Fame of the National Speakers Association.

Chad and his wife Shondell are the proud parents of four children. He enjoys quad rugby, hunting, fishing, traveling, and reading.

Visit Chad Hymas online at www.chadhymas.com

Introduction

By Chad's father, Kelly Hymas

You are about to embark on a journey as you read this work. However, you'll discover the journey you're reading is not the author's, nor is it mine or perhaps even yours. You may find that this writ is about someone else in your path that is in dire need of your ability and service. So, as you read within, please be willing to 'open up' your thought process. Think about those in your circle of influence, and those you have yet to meet, and then leave these pages with a greater desire to *"Do What Must Be Done"* and let your journey find its destiny! Take notes throughout. Write down your thoughts. Act on instinct. Again, *Do What Must Be Done.* Then watch the transformation unfold! For me, what has come to fruition in the last decade is nothing shy of a miracle. I sincerely wish the same results for you in your life.

*Chad with his dad,
Kelly Hymas*

Ten years ago, my wife Terrie and I were attending a national business convention in Dallas, Texas. We were awaiting the presentation of their keynote speaker. The gentleman was introduced as Hall of Fame Speaker Art Berg, a C-4 quadriplegic from Salt Lake City, Utah. Never in my life was I so moved as I was by Art Berg's presentation that day. I was so touched that when I returned home, I immediately contacted my children and told them I had obtained a video of Art's presentation and that we should all get together and watch it. Long story short, it never happened.

Three months later, my oldest son Chad was in an accident and was rendered a C-4 quadriplegic. Ironically, his circumstance was precisely the same as Art Berg, the gentleman whom we were so honored to hear that day.

My wife contacted Art's office to see if we could obtain other books or even videos that could help Chad during his rehabilitation. As fate would have it, and unbeknownst to us, those books and videos would be delivered to Chad's hospital room by Art Berg himself just days after our phone call to his office. Art, unannounced, appeared in Chad's hospital room. That day would change all of our lives FOREVER!

Prologue

Let me sleep. Just let me sleep. No. I can't. If I sleep, I will die.

Where am I? It's dark and deep. I can't breathe. Hay dust and exhaust fumes fill my nose and mouth. The chunka-chunka of an idling tractor breaks into my consciousness. I become aware that my face is smashed against metal and broken glass. The thick, salty taste of blood covers my swollen tongue.

I try to lift my hand to clear a way to breathe, but I can't find it. I can't find my hand. Where is my hand? I try to move, but the monstrous heel of some giant entity grinds my face against the control panel of my tractor. Confusion fills my mind. What happened?

"One. Two. Three. Four…" I have to count each breath or I will forget to breathe – and I will die. My face tingles. I fight to stay awake…

"Hi Chad."

She is beautiful. Sixteen years old. Tall and graceful with eyes that look into your soul and like what they see.

"Nice socks, Shondell."

What a dork! How could I ever get a girl like her by saying something stupid like that? Sure, I'm an athlete. I'm part of the "in crowd" and cool with my buddies. But with Shondell…

She just called and asked me out. She called me! She did for me what I could never have done. How could a "Chad" ever ask a "Shondell" to go out with him?

I gasp for breath. My head aches. My face hurts. The exhaust and hay dust is suffocating. I must breathe or die. I must remember to count. "One. Two. Three. Four…"

Moments ago, I was hastily loading a one-ton bale of hay with an old front-loader tractor. The hydraulics jerked spasmodically, making it difficult to secure the hay bale with the forks. I should have stopped and added hydraulic fluid. I didn't have time.

Heck, this has happened a dozen times before – a hundred times. I have horsed this machine into obedience every time and gotten away with it. I can always add fluid next time.

I was anxious to get home to see my son's first steps, but now there is a two thousand pound bale of hay on top of me, crushing the life out of me – and I am going nowhere.

Which is the dream? Which is real? Is this the dream? Please let this be the dream. No. The good stuff is the dream. The nightmare is reality.

"One. Two. Three…" If I just breathe long enough, I will sort this out and it will all be okay, right? Please, God, please let it be okay. I'm scared.

Shondell, where are you? My sweetheart. My boys. I don't want to die. "…Three. Four. Five…" I breathe as deeply as my bloody swollen lips and the crushing weight will allow. "…Six. Seven…"

"Catch, Dad!"

My three-year-old, Christian flings the orange foam ball wildly in my direction. I catch it expertly, whirl and slam-dunk it into the toy basketball net. Daddy is simply an amazing athlete. "Son, did you see how I did that? It's your turn, Christian. Go for it!" My handsome, magnificent, perfect Christian. The sun sparks off his golden hair. Sunburned nose, stubby fingers…

"Good boy! Hold your hands out. Here it comes. Good catch! Now, into the basket. I'll pick you up and you can dunk it. That's an assist son – a Daddy Assist – a new term in international sports. You made it! Yay! Two points!"

The calm blue sky, the soft orange ball, the bright green grass fade to shades of gray… "I don't feel so good, Christian. Go get Mom. Run, boy, run. I'll stay here and count. "Five. Six. Seven. Eight…" Hurry!

Fumes, dust, and pain assault my senses as I drift back into the nightmare that is my new reality. *Shondell, where are you?* I fight to breathe and keep my senses clear. "One. Two. Three. Four. Five…"

Kyler is almost here. My second son is about to be born.
"Count, Shondell. Relax, Honey. He'll be here soon. Breathe, Honey, breathe – the pain will ease if you just breathe – and count. One. Two. Three…"
He is finally here! Screaming a joyful protest to the world, his tiny fists clenched, eyes tightly closed…
The lights in the delivery room are too bright. They'll hurt my baby's eyes. "Turn them off…"

Oh, it's headlights. Shondell, Shondell, I'm over here! I'm still counting. I am counting – on you. Don't scream, Honey…

Dear God, Shondell needs your help. I need your help. Please don't take me from her. Don't take me from my boys. Please. My family needs me.

Don't take me – not yet.

"Simplify, simplify, simplify!"

~ Henry David Thoreau

One

Cut the Strings

6:30 p.m. Tuesday, April 3, 2001. A delicate spring evening. Lush irrigated alfalfa fields form vibrant green islands amidst an ocean of alkaline playa and sagebrush. The snow covered Onaqui mountains cast deep shadows across the semi-arid valley. The setting sun tints the slopes of the Oquirrh Mountains and fresh cumulous clouds in soft orange, purple and pink.

I don't really notice.

I am too busy succeeding.

I'm on my way home from a landscaping job. My cell phone rings with a special tone. It's Shondell. She programmed that unique ring, so I'd know it's her. Hearing it makes me smile. The excitement in her voice broadens my smile even more.

"Chad! Kyler just took his first steps! Hurry home so you can see him walk."

"Okay, Honey, warm up the camcorder. I'm on my way. I have to stop and feed the elk first, 'kay?" I feed the elk every night. Shondell knows my routine – fortunately for me.

My dusty, dark green, '95 Dodge Ram roars down the gravel road to a field north of the house and skids to a stop. Like a Pony Express rider changing horses, I jump out of the truck and hop onto my old tractor. It's unbalanced. The hydraulic arms and forks make it top-heavy. It bucks, bounces, and sways as I drive it to a nearby haystack.

Like a hungry Brontosaurus, the hydraulic arms stretch fifteen feet into the evening sky and slide steel forks under a one-ton bale of hay at the top of the pile. As I manipulate the hydraulic controls to lift the monster bale clear, the greasy black hydraulic hoses spasm. The forks holding the bale fail. The bale falls back onto the stack.

It's low on hydraulic fluid. I know it. It's obvious. But it's a simple fix; remedied in six or seven minutes. Just go to the shed only fifty feet away. Grab a can of fluid. Fill the hydraulic reservoir. *Done* and ready to go. Safe *and* smart.

But that will take too long. I want to see my one-year-old take his first steps.

Tractor with fallen bale of hay

Try again. If finesse won't do it, force will. I yank on the lever. This time, the starving hydraulic system jerks the forks upward. The huge bale breaks free and rolls backwards, falling toward me. My first instinct is to lean back out of the way. For some reason, I duck forward instead. If I had pulled back, it would have been all over but the burying. There is a metal wedge behind the seat, and I would have been cut in half.

The bale's crushing weight lands fully on me, slamming my face into the control panel. My body goes instantly numb and limp. I can't feel my feet, legs, hands – nothing. The only movement possible is a slight shrug of my shoulders.

I am paralyzed.

Pinned under two thousand pounds of alfalfa, I am alone in the growing darkness, struggling for breath. The laboring tractor engine spews exhaust fumes into my limited air-space through the cracked sides of the crushed exhaust pipe.

Unable to move or help myself, fear – real fear – begins to overwhelm my thoughts. Fear of death, fear of paralysis, fear of tomorrow.

Fear that I will die.

Fear that I won't.

The giant bale of hay crushes my mouth and nose against the dash. I can barely breathe, but barely is better than not at all. Breathe. Just breathe. I scrape my teeth against my lips to force open a bigger gap. I don't care about the blood. I only care about air. *I want to live.*

Fear and fatigue compete for top billing. Heart-pounding panic takes the lead, then overwhelming sleepiness from carbon monoxide poisoning. Sleep. Irresistible sleep. A place of no pain.

I slip in and out of consciousness.

It grows darker; I grow weaker. Shondell will show up soon. I know it. Too much time has passed since I promised to be home. We had a "discussion" about that yesterday. A "discussion" she won.

Will Shondell expect me to keep my word about spending more time with our family by getting home before she puts the boys to bed? She made me promise. I promised. Does she believe I will keep my promise this time? I hope so.

She will wonder where I am. She will know something is wrong and will come looking for me. Sure she will. She might wait a little, though, to see if I'll keep my promise. Oh, please don't wait, Shondell. Can I hang on long enough?

For the first time in my life, I can do nothing for myself. Nothing, except stay alive. Nothing, except breathe, count, count, breathe, breathe. I am terrified of what being paralyzed means. If my request to live is granted, it may mean a life of pain and difficulty; but my family – Shondell, Christian, little Kyler – is on the other side of that pain – and they need me. They can't make it without me.

What I am about to learn, however, is how much *I* need *them* – have *always* needed them – and that *I* can't make it without *them*.

I must face this fear and pain if I am going to stay with my family. I pray. Somehow, now, it seems easier to breathe. I tense up, start to suffocate, pray again, relax a little, and breathe a little easier. I am getting dizzy. I fade in and out, but counting my breaths helps me stay focused and breathing – and alive.

What can you do when you think you can do nothing? You can do something. Focus on the goal – life. Mind the task at hand – the one thing I can do, the only thing I can do – breathe.

…Five. Six. Seven. Eight. Nine. Ten... Twenty. Twenty-one. Twenty two… Thirty-three…Forty… The sun sets. The sky darkens. The desert air chills. I grow weaker.

I pray more fervently that I am allowed to live. The sound of the struggling tractor engine becomes a distant white noise as I focus on doing what needs to be done. Breathe – just breathe.

Shondell driving up in the car

Headlights reflecting off the gravel below let me know Shondell is finally here. It felt like an eternity, but she is finally here. I allow myself to feel excitement – and hope. *She found me. I'm going to make it.*

Her car skids to a stop, she kills the engine and throws open the door. I hear her feet crunch on the gravel as she races to the tractor.

She calls my name repeatedly, frantically. I can't respond. I blink my eyes to let her know I am alive, but there is no light for her to see my cue. She reaches under the bale of hay and touches my face. When her fingers touch my cheek, I feel cold and unresponsive to her. She cries out and runs back to the car – then turns and runs back to me. What is she doing? She is screaming, that's for sure – but in the midst of her anxiety and abject fear, she has the presence of mind to turn off the tractor engine. Fresh air! What a relief!

I hear the car door slam again, the car engine roars back to life and the spurt of gravel from the spinning wheels. The headlight glare rotates in a wild half-circle and fades away as Shondell races for help.

When Shondell reached up to touch my face, she inadvertently cleared an airway through the suffocating hay. With the engine off and the fumes abating, I get some fresh air. It revives me for a moment, but only for a moment. A tingling sensation envelops my face. The dizziness returns. I begin counting again. "One. Two. Three. Four…"

I don't know how much time passes. It seems like days. Then the dull reflection of red and blue flashing lights on the gravel tells me help has finally arrived.

Police, ambulance and firefighters arriving

The first police officer reaches under the one-ton bale of hay and attempts to lift it off of me. Of course, it doesn't budge. He grabs his flashlight and shines it under the hay into my face. I blink. He yells over his shoulder to his partner, "He's alive! He's alive! Help me move the hay."

Even working together two officers can't move it – not a fraction of an inch. A thousand pounds each? Of course they can't move it.

"Cut the strings," I whisper. My voice is weak. They can't hear me.

I am not going to last much longer. If they will just cut the strings, the bale will break apart, and they can drag me out of here.

"Lift, Joe, lift!"

"Just cut the strings," I mumble, "Please cut the strings."

"C'mon harder."

"It's too heavy! We can't lift it. We gotta go for help! Hang on Chad, we'll be right back!"

I am alone again in the growing darkness. Wonderful painless, peaceful, irresistible sleep beckons. I struggle to remain conscious. One. Two. Three. Four... Where are they? How long does it take for police, fire, ambulance, to arrive? Where is the Coast Guard? Where are the Marines? Where is that one old farmer with enough common sense to *just cut the strings?*

The desert air grows chilly as the sky darkens. I grow weaker. Dizziness overcomes me and I begin to drift off into that gray space somewhere between the living and the dead.

Help finally arrives. One of the police officers bends down so I can see his face. "Hold on! A fire engine is here. There are six men aboard."

I do the math. Two big, strong cops and six burly firemen must move a ton of dead weight off me. That's two hundred forty five pounds each. No way can they possibly do that – but somehow, miraculously, they do. A couple of neighbors who have arrived at the scene stand by to catch me. They lower my limp body to the ground where I lie in a broken heap.

Why didn't they cut the strings? They could have saved a long, tortured hour.

How heavy is hay? A piece of hay is about the weight of a feather. How many pieces of hay does it take to make two thousand pounds? Lots. That package of sixteen bazillion individual pieces of hay wrapped in a gigantic bundle is a crushing weight. But separated, it would have been nothing. I feel bad saying this, because it makes me sound ungrateful – and I am *very* grateful to the guys who saved my life that night – but there is a point to be made here, isn't there?

Is it too big?

Is it overwhelming?

Cut the strings – just cut the strings!

Are you buried under crushing burdens? Projects that are too huge? Schedules that are too complicated? Maybe you are trying to do too much at once – trying to do *every*thing instead of doing *some*thing.

Cut the strings and cut yourself free. Do one thing at a time – and get it *DOne*. Move "out of the strain of the doing into the peace of the done."1

---

1 "Out of the strain of the Doing, into the peace of the Done." *~Julia Louise Woodruff*

Today is the last day
of the first of your life.

~ Chad Hymas

Two

The Calm Before the Storm

Before I meet Shondell, I hardly ever date the same girl twice. Then Shondell invites me out. I've never spoken to her, except once to comment on the purple socks she was wearing. But I know who she is. She is smart, beautiful and popular. Everyone likes her.

What a great surprise it is when Shondell calls me up and asks me out. It is November 18, 1991 – my eighteenth birthday. I pick up the phone and here is this sweet voice – this amazing girl – asking me out! She asks me if I'd go to the high school play with her. What a birthday present!

She asks me to get the tickets.

Of course, I will.

She asks me to pick her up.

So I do.

Chad and Shondell, dating

If she asks me to bring her the moon in a fruit basket, I will do that, too. I don't realize it, but I am a husband in training.

I have a job at a movie theater, which means many late nights for me. After work, I often stop by Shondell's house. Sometimes, I wake her up and we talk. Other times, I just leave little treats or mementos for her. One time, I sneak into her house (her mom lets me in) and quietly scatter rose petals all over her room while she sleeps.

In June, 1992, I turn in my papers to volunteer to serve a two-year mission for my church. I wait anxiously. It doesn't take long, but for an eighteen-year-old, it seems like forever.

Finally, the envelope arrives. I will be going to Bangkok, Thailand. I am excited, yet apprehensive. I'll be gone for two years – away from everything and everyone that is familiar – especially Shondell.

They say this kind of separation will make or break a relationship. But it makes ours. We communicate through letters and audiotapes, sharing our hopes and dreams.

Missionaries and soldiers often receive a dreaded "Dear John" letter, letting them know the girl they left behind is tired of waiting and is moving on. The thought of getting such a letter from Shondell strikes fear in my heart. But as the months pass, those worries fade away. Sure glad my name isn't John!

Our mutual interest in discovering what is important to each other and our positive, supportive correspondence secures our relationship. Shondell has the unique ability to help me maintain focus on what is important and is a wonderful asset to my missionary work.

Sharing spiritual messages is only one aspect of my mission. Rebuilding bamboo homes torn apart by monsoon is another way I help these beautiful people survive and prosper in their humble circumstances. It humbles me. I gain deep appreciation for the noble spirit of these valiant people. Truly on my own for the first time in my young life, I am called on to help families and sometimes, entire villages. I learn greater focus and dedication. I learn the value of simple things – daily work habits, work ethic, etc. Most important, I discover the power of doing little things every day that add up to getting *DOne* the big things that change lives.

I return from Bangkok on November 11, 1994. Nothing has changed, yet everything has changed. We have grown and matured, but we did it together, so we didn't grow apart. Eight hundred days of growth for both of us. Now here we are, different but the same. The same sweethearts, but even stronger friends.

Things pick up right where we left off. Soon, we can hardly remember being separated – because, in effect, we never were.

On Christmas Eve, 1994, Shondell goes to the mall with her mom, her sister, Jennilyn and her two-year-old nephew, Bradley. They tell her I am busy at the theater and will meet them later. Jennilyn heads for the middle of the mall, so Bradley can see Santa. There is a long line of parents, grandparents and children waiting to see the jolly elf in the red suit. Jennilyn grabs Shondell's hand and pulls her toward the front of the line.

"What are you doing?" Shondell protests, "Everyone is staring at us. I know you are excited for Bradley to see Santa, but let's wait our turn."

Jennilyn ignores Shondell's protest and drags her along. One of Santa's elves gives Shondell a knowing look, "Hello, little girl. Are you here to see Santa?"

"Ho, ho, ho!" says Santa, "Come here, little girl."

Two suspiciously tall elves grab her hands and pull her to Santa. Shondell is dying of embarrassment, but beginning to suspect that something is up.

"Have you been a good little girl this year? What would you like for Christmas?" Santa asks.

"I don't know," Shondell answers coyly. "Is there something I should ask for?"

Santa says, "Well, how about this?" He points to the side of his throne at a little green, red and white striped house.

I appear in the doorway of the little house, festively attired in a belted green tunic, long striped stockings (spray painted leotards) and pointed boots ("customized" cowboy boots). I get on one knee in front of two hundred laughing, cheering Christmas Eve shoppers, and say, "Shondell, will you marry me?"

She doesn't answer; she just starts crying. I'm not sure if she is crying because I look like an idiot or because her heart is touched, but I take her tears as a "yes."

Four months after my return, Shondell and I are married and begin the life we have dreamed of.

Wedding day!

With my two younger brothers' help, I establish a landscaping business and build it into a profitable venture. Planting trees and flowers, building waterfalls, putting in sprinkler systems – getting my hands dirty while creating beauty – gives me great satisfaction. Business is great. Life is great.

For our first couple of years together, we live in a little apartment in West Valley City, Utah. Shondell is a great support to me as I build my business. She supports me in my every dream or ambition. Her job as a paralegal allows me the time I need to establish my clientele. She works for two and a half years while I get the business going.

When our son Kelly Christian Hymas is born, Shondell stops. She feels her place is at home with our son. I agree. It is the right decision for us.

As my landscaping business becomes more profitable, Shondell and I are able to build our dream home on ranch property in Rush Valley, one hour west of Salt Lake City. We move into our new home in June, 1999.

Our second son, Kyler Chase, is born six months later, just two days before Christmas. What a great Christmas present! My two beautiful children, Christian and Kyler, are a great joy to my wife and me. All of our dreams are coming true.

When it becomes legal to raise elk in Utah, we start an elk ranch with forty head we move in from Colorado. This project is something my dad and I have talked about for years.

Life moves along smoothly. True, navigating life's stormy waters with its currents and undercurrents of parenting problems, health hazards, taxes and terrorists, is more involved than it was in high school, but it's still pretty simple. I have two wonderful kids and an incredible wife. My parents, who taught me well and endowed me with a strong work ethic, are still around to help. Mom loves being a grandma and helps out with the kids. Dad pitches in and helps me with my business whenever I need him. Life is good for our young family. We are happy. Looks like smooth sailing from here to the horizon, but it is just the calm before the storm.

Always focused on my job, striving to build security for my family and success for myself, I often leave for work in the morning before my boys wake up and come home after they are in bed. This happens a lot. It is not a good thing.

Shondell often protests, "Chad, business is going well. Can't you spend more time at home?"

I say yes.

But I don't do it.

"All I have seen teaches me to trust the creator
for all I have not seen."

~ Ralph Waldo Emerson

Three

Shondell Remembers

Chad and I have a little argument.

It is April 2nd, seven years and two children into our marriage. We don't speak to one another for three hours. It is a typical husband and wife disagreement. Husband is wrong. Wife is right.

It is about him not getting home early enough to be with his family before the kids go to bed. Chad promises to do better, much better. He assures me I am right and thanks me for caring. The problem seems resolved, but since we so rarely fight, it is unsettling to me.

Please understand. Chad is a true family man in the best sense of the word. He is an awesome dad. He loves his children and they love him. He plays with them. He listens to them. Chad is not working to stay away from his family; he is working to create a financial foundation that will support his family. Chad has always been a hard worker. He gets more done by doing every day what needs to be done – not just talking about it. So, it is understandable that his "always doing" to get things *done* sometimes leave important things *un*done. He just needs a reminder. I am his wife. I'll remind him. That is my job!

The next day starts out great. Chad is apologetic. Chad is sweet. Chad is attentive. He tells me he loves me and, best of all, he tells me why. He reminds me how beautiful and smart I am (look how smart *he* is). Then he goes off to work.

He phones several times to say he loves me. Twice he calls to tell me to turn on the radio because one of our special songs is playing. I am beginning to think maybe a good fight once every two or three years is a good idea – especially when it gets me this kind of attention!

Late that afternoon, I phone Chad. I am excited about Kyler taking his first steps. There are certain moments that should be celebrated in one's life. A child's first step is one such moment. We cherished the experience of watching Christian take his first steps. We videoed, we photographed – I swear we almost called the *Boston Daily Herald* to herald it. Now it is Kyler's turn. When I tell Chad the news, he says, "Perfect! Now we can play basketball "two-on-two" rather than "two-on-one.""

Chad tells me he has to stop and feed the elk before he comes home, but hastily assures me he'll hurry.

Usually he stops by the house and takes Christian with him. Christian stands on the side of the tractor while Daddy loads up the hay to feed the elk. Sometimes, he sits on his daddy's lap to "help" him drive. I don't even want to think what might have happened, if he was with his dad when that bale of hay broke loose. But on this particular day, Chad goes to the field without Christian. He is in a hurry to get home to see Kyler walk. I look out the window and see Chad about a mile from the house, driving out to the field to feed the elk.

I often play a game with the kids while we wait for Daddy to come home. We look out the window facing the road. If we can't see Chad, we dash into the master bedroom and look out that window. Back and forth we run, checking one window and then the other, until we finally see him. The boys giggle and squeal at the fun of this game.

He doesn't come home. By eight o'clock, I assume he's gotten started on some project or another and it is taking more time than he expected. Chad does that a lot.

I keep looking out the window. I figure he is working on sprinklers, or something like that, so I am not really worried. I am getting a little peeved, though, considering his promise of the night before.

As it grows darker, a nagging concern begins to build in a corner of my mind. There are no lights. It is dark enough now that he would need lights, whatever he is doing. Why can't I see any lights?

About 8:15, I decide to go up there and nag at him for being late – again! I have a wonderful speech prepared. It is short, not particularly sweet. "You said you'd be home and you're not."

Leaving dinner simmering on the stove, I put the kids in the car. As we get close to where he is working, I can see the tractor by the haystack. Then I see that huge bale of hay on top of the tractor. I can't see Chad. A horrible feeling sweeps over me. Fear. Incredible fear. Fear so strong it hurts.

I shove the gas pedal to the floor and speed up to the tractor, slam on the brakes, skidding to a halt. I kill the engine, cram on the emergency brake and jump out, my heart in my throat. I run around the car and over to the tractor.

Chad is pinned under that massive bale of hay. I can see part of his back and shoulders, but nothing else. I reach up to feel his face. It feels cold and unresponsive. I try to look up under the bale, but can't see anything except that his shoulders are moving a little. Is he trying to tell me he is alive, or are these just involuntary muscle spasms? I am frantic with fear.

I jump back in the car. Then I get out again. I don't want to leave him. I run back and turn off the tractor engine, and stand there for a moment, confused and frightened.

I need help, and I need it fast. I get in the car and barrel back down the road. "Hold on, Christian. Hold on." I say, over and over again. My tears make it difficult to see.

"I'm holding on, Mama."

Dashing into the house, I grab the phone and, with shaking hands, dial 911 and tell dispatch what has happened. "Don't hang up," an official voice says calmly. "You need to help me guide the officers. Watch out the window and tell me when they get to the right road."

Christian hugs my leg, trying to comfort me, "It's okay, Mama. It's okay." He doesn't know what is going on, but he knows something is. He keeps saying over and over. "It's okay, Mama. It will be okay."

Angels speak through children sometimes, but I am not listening. I am trying to keep calm for the sake of the kids. It isn't working.

Finally, the police car comes into view. "They're at the corner," I fairly shout into the poor man's ear. "Go right."

"We got it, ma'am," the officer tells me. And I hang up.

I quickly call Chad's dad, then run with my boys back to the car and speed back to Chad. I arrive just as they lift the bale of hay off my husband. I watch horrified as he is lowered to the ground. Is he alive?

I can't keep from crying. This is all so horrible. Recalling that scene still makes me tremble. I can't bring myself to watch the reenactment video they've made, especially the part showing me driving up that road. I try to stay calm for my children's sake – and for my husband's. I can't hold it in. I begin to weep.

Thirty or forty people mill around, shouting instructions or questions, calling for this or that. Rush Valley is so small that when there is a 911 call, everyone hears it on their scanners and bands together to help – volunteer firefighters, deputies, neighbors, everyone.

Someone is getting ready to cut a hole in Chad's throat so he can breathe better. DeAnn Evans, a neighbor, also a nurse, stops them. She is kneeling beside Chad as he whispers, "DeAnn. Let me talk. I can breathe. Tell everyone 'Be quiet.' I know what I need. I know what's wrong."

DeAnn tells everyone to quiet down and listen.

You can hear Chad's whisper move across the desert floor, "I can breathe. I don't need a 'trach'. What I need is a blessing, and someone to take care of Shondell."

They put my husband in an ambulance to stabilize him while waiting for a Life Flight helicopter. DeAnn asks everyone to stop for a moment. Grant Smith, a volunteer firefighter, several medical technicians, and other neighbors who attend our church gather around Chad and give him a blessing.

With aching tears in my throat, I climb into the ambulance and kneel beside my husband. I put my hand on his unresponsive arm. "I've heard what they are saying, Honey; you have no feeling anywhere. You will be going in for immediate surgery. I don't know how you'll end up, Sweetheart, but promise me you'll fight to stay with us. Promise me! Stay alive. We'll make everything else work."

"I will," he whispers. "I will."

LifeFlight taking off

With a powerful, comforting "whoosh," salvation lands in the field. They carry my husband, now strapped onto a stretcher, into the waiting helicopter, and fly away into the dark.

"When a broken bone heals,
it is stronger in that place
than it was before the break.

It is the same with mental
or emotional injury and healing.

You can become stronger than before the injury.
That is the beauty of healing.
That is the gift of injury."

~ *Chad Hymas*

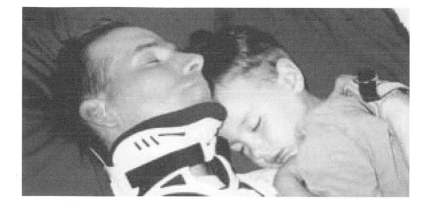

Four

Brave New World

I struggle to breathe. I slip in and out of consciousness, groggy from pain medication, unable to fully understand what has happened. I see bright glittering stars in front of me. They are so real, so close. I can reach right out and touch them.

Gradually the painkillers wear off. I become coherent, but can't communicate. I am hungry, but can't eat. A plastic tube snakes down my throat. Other tubes run up my nose, down the back of my throat and into my stomach or directly into my arm with a needle. One supplies my body with food, another with liquid.

Wires twist over my face. A machine helps me breathe. I am frightened and in pain – but no pain below my upper chest. That frightens me even more. I feel a burning dry thirst and a constant sense of suffocation. Even with the help of a mechanical respirator, I struggle for each shallow breath.

A "halo brace" holds my head immobile. There is nothing angelic about this halo brace. Four screws have been drilled through my skin and into my skull, two on each side above the ears. The pain is excruciating. The foundation of the brace is a large plastic breastplate lined with sheepskin to keep the plastic from irritating my skin. Steel bars are attached to the breastplate, extend up and over my shoulders, and are fastened to the back. The halo brace is connected to weights that hold my head and neck straight and keep pressure off my spine. It allows me to move nothing but my eyes.

My family is gathered around my bed. Shondell is holding my hand. I can't feel it, but I can feel *her*. Mom, Dad and his wife, Terrie; my brothers, Brian and Jeremy; Shondell's father, Joe; her brothers, Ryan and Matthew; and her sisters, Jennilyn and Alisa. They are all with me.

They are ready to hear the worst.

I am not.

Three doctors step into the room. They have assessed my injuries and are ready to report their findings.

The damage to my spine is extensive. Three vertebrae, C3, C4 and C5 are fractured. They made a six-inch incision in my neck and inserted a titanium plate. My neck is not paralyzed and the stitches are beginning to burn. Bone has been removed from my right hip to repair the fractured vertebrae.

They are unsure of the prognosis for my spinal cord. It's obviously traumatized or damaged. It may be severed, or nearly so, and I will likely be in a wheelchair for the rest of my life. It could be just kinked and eventually straighten itself out. In that case, I could possibly walk again.

For now, I have lost the use of my legs and all of my stomach muscles, so I can't sit up on my own or have any reasonable semblance of balance. I've lost two of the three major muscles in my chest, but I still have diaphragm control, which is why I can breathe, albeit barely. My ability to cough or sneeze is gone.

What about bladder control? Or bowel control? The muscles that control those functions are useless as well. Why is this important? When quadriplegics and paraplegics are asked what they miss most, is it intimacy? Nope. Bladder control. Bowel control. Who wants to wear diapers!

I have lost all feeling and function in my arms, hands and fingers. I am officially a quadriplegic – all four limbs permanently or temporarily – paralyzed.

My eyes are all I can move. I look at each family member. They try to hide their concern and fear. They are unsuccessful. It is difficult for them to digest such tough information. It is hard not to cry.

There is some good news. If my spinal cord isn't severed, I should regain some important functions. "In that case," the doctors tell me, "you will eventually have use of your wrists."

"Big deal," I think to myself.

Well, it *is* a big deal. Anything, when you have nothing, is a big deal. A few weeks later, this prediction comes true. I cannot feel my wrists, but I can move them. Over the years, this has allowed me significant and important function. Wrist movement gives me great advantage when putting on my shoes, buttering a roll – writing a book. One simple function, a 1% improvement, can create 1000% improvement in my quality of life and ultimate independence.

The doctors predict I will regain the function of my biceps. A couple of months later, this becomes reality. This is the only usable muscle group I have in my upper arms. I have no triceps function, but I have perfect shoulders and fairly impressive 'guns.' The miners I speak to regularly are quite impressed when I flex; and my kids pretend to be scared!

One in four chest muscles works. A wonderful one in four. The muscle that is unaffected is my diaphragm. That one muscle allowed me to count my breaths or, rather, gave me breaths to count during those fifty minutes or so while I was trapped under that bale of hay. It is still the only muscle in my chest that works.

The doctors continue, "You'll be confined to an electric wheelchair. You will learn to operate it by using your wrist or your chin. And one more thing, your body's thermostat does not work anymore. You've lost essential control of body temperature. You have to understand that quadriplegics die easily from heatstroke or hypothermia in circumstances that would merely make others sweat or shiver. You can't shiver – nor can you sweat. You won't be able to enjoy the outdoors the way you have."

Hunting, fishing, skiing, snowmobiling and other outdoor sports have always been a major part of my life. It is an important part of my relationship with my brothers and my dad. I catch my father's gaze. Our eyes lock for a heartbeat. Then I look away. Hot tears trickle from the corners of my eyes and run down the sides of my face. It is impossible to comprehend that this is my new life. Questions swirl through my mind. Can I still be a husband? A father? What about athletics? What about the elk farm? My landscaping business?

As if reading my thoughts, one of the doctors gently informs me it will no longer be possible for me to run my businesses.

My brothers chime in, "Doctor, you're dead wrong. Chad can still run the business. He never got out of the truck, anyway!"

I fire them on the spot!

We've always joked around and, even in this terrible situation, we see no need to stop. In fact, humor is a big part of what saves me.

Other thoughts vie for my attention. How will I coach my boys? My father coached me in basketball and baseball when I was a little kid. I loved it. I've always wanted to do the same for my boys – maybe even coach their Little League teams when they get older.

How can that now be possible?

Can I make love to my wife? Can I even court her in any way that is remotely romantic?

How will I... How could I... How can I – be me?

Darkness rolls into my soul as evening fog rolls into a darkening valley. I give in to tears. I am hurt, bewildered, and impotent. My soul is in anguish. On top of it all, I am humiliated, because I just can't stop crying.

Determine never to be idle.
No person will have occasion to complain of the
want of time who never loses any.
It is wonderful how much may be done,
if we are always doing.

~Thomas Jefferson

Five

A Tragic Blessing

A Mother's Perspective

It is a night like any other. I'm watching the ten o'clock news, waiting for David Letterman to come on. My daughter will be home from work soon. I am surprised when my sons Jeremy and Brian quietly walk in.

They have that look. Mothers know "that look." Mothers dread "that look." Something is wrong – very wrong. A million questions collide in my mind, but I can only ask, "Who?"

"Mom, it's Chad. There's been an accident. We need to get to the hospital – now."

The twenty-minute ride feels like twenty eternities. Little is said. We know Chad is badly hurt, but we have no details. Curled up in the back seat – I pray. How do you pray about what you do not know? You only know that God knows – so you pray.

Some say not knowing is the worst part. I used to think so, too. But after finding out what happened and, assuming what the future is likely to be for my son and his young family, I prefer not knowing – not now, not ever.

At the hospital, we walk quickly to the emergency room desk. They are expecting us. Not a good sign. Two men in white suits and white ties lead us to a quiet room – decorated in white. Classic chairs, lamps, end tables, rug, everything – white.

"What a lovely room," I think. Then it hits me. We are in a chapel. The chapel is designed to remind us of the peace of heaven. That sudden realization is anything but peaceful.

"The doctors will be here to speak with you soon."

That's all these men say, but that says a lot – and it is terrifying. They hesitate and look at each other. Not knowing what else to say, they quietly turn and leave.

Alone in that white room, we stand silent, mute.

Long minutes pass. Two doctors push open the door and invade our sanctuary. Gently, authoritatively, one of them says, "Your son, Chad, is alive, but barely. His neck is broken. He needs surgery." We are told, however, that surgery has to be held off for twenty-four hours to wait for the swelling to go down in his neck.

I don't hear much more of that conversation. I am in shock. Disbelief fights the facts.

In the Intensive Care Unit, Chad is telling his brothers what needs to be done for their landscaping clients. Paralyzed, in shock and pain, Chad is still getting things done. Barely audible, he is assigning his brothers, who have been his right and left hands for the past two years, a list of tasks, complete with names and phone numbers of who-needs-what, from memory. That is my Chad; always doing.

Chad says, "What can you do, when you can do nothing? You can do *something*." And that he is doing.

The next days and weeks are… I am searching for a word that means more than "hard" or "difficult." "Impossible" "tragic" "hopeless" "unreal" "unbearable" "torturous" just don't cut it. How about mixing all those words together and pouring them into my heart?

Chad has always been active, athletic, full of life. Now I don't even know if he will have a life. But a mother's job is to hope – and I do my job.

These first few days are the worst. His head is screwed into this painful, but necessary, thing called a "halo brace" – and it is bolted to the wall. It is more than I can stand to see, but stand it I must – with a smile – for him.

Flat on his back, Chad strains to see who has come into his room. I say, "Hi, Hon." His silence scares me. Then I understand. He was having trouble breathing so they inserted a lubricated breathing tube down his throat. A mixed blessing. Feeling suffocated in order to breathe. That tube helps him breathe but stops him from speaking. The small percentage of his body that he can move, his head and shoulders, are immobilized and even his voice is silenced. Now he can do nothing but think. He is locked in his mind. He can't respond in any way.

Chad's eyes speak fury.

Each time I see him, he gives me such a look. He can only convey his unspoken, perhaps unspeakable, thoughts with angry eyes.

He just lies there, staring at the ceiling, his head literally screwed to the wall. What must be going through his mind? I don't know. I am not sure I want to know. My son, once the master of getting things done, can't do anything. He can't even give direction or instruction. He cannot speak, his paralyzed hands cannot write. His life, as he knows it, as we know it, is over.

He will be in a wheelchair the rest of his days – assuming he lives. He will rely on others for everything – getting dressed, bathing, brushing his teeth, combing his hair, shaving, working, driving… well, everything. He will always be dependent on someone to take care of even his most intimate and personal needs.

Chad has always been the provider. But that is over. Now, he will always need his family to provide for him. How can he ever run a business? Support his family? I can't even imagine the turmoil he must be going through.

Being in the hospital is tough, but when Chad comes home, his real struggles begin. My son's family and community have banded together to try and make life at home easier for him. They have removed rugs and some carpets so his wheelchair can roll easier. They have built a ramp in front of his house, making it wheelchair accessible.

Later they will build a deck so he can move around the outside of his home and hopefully feel some sense of connection with his beloved ranch. They will also remodel the shower in the master bathroom – expanding it to accommodate a bathing chair. The counter and sinks will be lowered and the cabinet below taken out to accommodate his knees.

We hoped that once he came home and settled into his new life, he would, at least, be comfortable and content. We were wrong. Though Chad really appreciates our efforts, my son has never been content with comfortable or comfortable with content. He is always doing and getting things done.

While he was in the hospital, Chad's number one desire was to get home. Perhaps you have heard it said, "Wanting is often better than having." In this case, it is true. Being home only reminds Chad of everything he can no longer do. He can only sit on the sidelines and watch everyone else do what he had done just a few short weeks ago.

He goes to the hospital often, for physical therapy, yes, but also because he feels at home there. He wants to be with his new friends – other patients confined to wheelchairs. They are like him. In that safe place, there are no haunting reminders of all he has lost.

Here with Misti, his physical therapist, there is praise and encouragement for simple accomplishments. It isn't the praise he needs; it is the understanding of what it takes to get things done, when one can do so little. It is her understanding of how something as simple as picking up a fork (which takes him several minutes and unbelievable concentration) is such a big deal – such an accomplishment. He still can't brush his teeth, shave or dress himself. Those little things are on his list of "big things I gotta do."

This is Chad's world now. The one he is comfortable in. That other life no longer exists for him. He doesn't want it to. It is much too painful for him to see the dream he has built, yet is no longer a part of.

After a long month in ICU and Rehab, my son finally gets his own room. He can breathe and swallow on his own. That's about it. He has a loyal family who would gladly take care of him for the rest of his life – but he doesn't want that.

What's next? Advance from working to survive to working to succeed. Success, as it often does, comes in small steps. In Chad's case, baby steps – literally. He has to learn *again* to sit up on his own, eat with a spoon, and drink from a cup. Chad says it's relearning the life skills of a two-year-old, and asks me to help. I ask him how. He reminds me that I am his mom; that I taught him once and I can teach him again.

Freedom and mobility are critically important to Chad. He must learn to get around in a wheelchair. My neighbor, Susan Bale, a registered nurse (RN) tells me how impossible this is for someone with Chad's level of paralysis – but not for someone with his level of determination.

In the beginning, he sits for hours at a time, trying to move his wheelchair past a strip of tape on the floor only four inches ahead. This is incredibly difficult, because he has nothing much to work with. He has yet to develop the use of his wrists and biceps. All he has are shoulders and arms, stiffened against their joints, to manipulate the wheels of the chair. In addition he has only, maybe, seven percent of the strength he had before the accident. It will take days – practicing two hours at a time – to be able to push his chair a few inches, then a foot or two, then a yard. Finally, after a week or so, he manages to navigate the length of the hall – about 50 feet.

Often, I walk with my son as he makes his torturously slow daily journey down the hall.

Chad has been in the hospital now for several weeks and, while making his practice rounds, has met nearly everyone, and knows them by name. There is a young bicyclist (we'll call him Peter) who was hit by an automobile. He suffered extensive brain injury. Peter's body healed, but his brain did not.

We pass Peter and his mother. She is walking him even more slowly in the same direction we are going. We stop to exchange pleasantries then move on. It is heart wrenching. Her son has healed physically, but not mentally. He is mostly unresponsive. Peter no longer seems to be the son she raised and for whom she, like any mother, had such hopes and dreams. Peter drags alongside his mom, apparently with no idea of where he is or even who he is. He doesn't know what happened. He doesn't know that anything has happened. I silently wonder whether it would be better to be paralyzed physically or to suffer such severe brain dysfunction.

Quietly, Chad answers my unspoken question. "It could be worse, Mom. I would rather have my body paralyzed than my mind."

"Yes, you say that," I think, "but Peter hasn't the capacity to understand what he has lost or to worry about the future. You know what happened and what you have lost. Are you really better off?"

But I keep my thoughts to myself.

My concerns seem to be validated after Chad gets home from the hospital. With no professional staff to help him, he must rely on family, especially his wife, for everything. He hates the fact that Shon must do everything for him. In the privacy of their home, I hear Chad say – and he says it more than once – "I didn't marry you so you'd have to take care of me!" He is the husband. He is the father. He is the provider. He is supposed to take care of his family. *He* is supposed to take care of *her*.

His moods grow darker.

As if Chad and Shon don't have enough to deal with, the doctors tell this young, scared couple that most marriages don't survive this kind of devastation. Why? Because the healthy spouse leaves the injured one? No. It's the other way around. The one in the wheelchair pushes the other one away.

They are no different – that is, Chad isn't.

Several months after the accident, Chad is having a bad day and he is so unable to do a thing about... well, much of anything.

I am in the kitchen. They are in the bedroom. Chad's voice can be heard throughout the house. He is asking Shon – no, he is ordering her – to get him in his wheelchair, get him in the van, so he can get out of here. He wants to leave. Forever. Permanently gone – so she can have a life. His life is over. Hers doesn't have to be. She doesn't need a wreck of a husband – a crippled, useless...

He can't drive himself. He can't even get in the van by himself. He wants to go away. Somewhere. Anywhere. He needs Shon to help him get in the van so he can get out of there. He is insistent. Frustrated. Angry. My heart is breaking. I cannot interfere. I hear

Shon crying softly, refusing to help him. Finally, her voice firms. Gently and clearly, she says, "No, Chad. I will not help you leave me."

They are joined at the heart – but in this moment, all my son feels is that he is no good for anything or to anyone. Not for his family and especially not for his beautiful wife. Not financially, not physically, and not emotionally. He believes he cannot make her happy – and it is killing him to think that he is, and always will be, responsible for her unhappiness.

Chad needs to feel useful – no, he needs to *be* useful – working and contributing. He isn't.

Then his good friend, Lee Johnson, steps in. He hires Chad to work for him at Broken Arrow, a local construction company. This small act of kindness is a life-changing event. Lee's original intent was just to get Chad out of the house – away from the reminders of what once was – and move forward towards something, anything – even if that "anything" is being an office clerk.

Getting back to the basics of life and business seems a pretty good place to start. Simple tasks done consistently and well have always been Chad's style. Intuitively, he knows the importance of doing the little things that bring ultimate success. Lee's blessing to Chad is giving him an opportunity to realize he could apply those same principles to getting things done, though perhaps differently.

Six months after Lee hires him, Chad is asked to speak at a local church. They wheel him to the side of the pulpit where they rigged a microphone at his level.

He tells his story – simply, frankly, and honestly. Afterwards, someone asks him what he would charge to speak to his company.

Chad doesn't know what to say. This is not a common situation for my son. He has never been asked what he would charge to speak. As far as I know, this is the first time he has spoken publicly about his situation. I am sure it never occurred to him that he could do this professionally.

A simple beginning for an inspiring career. Chad moves many with his heartfelt story. He is an inspirational speaker already, and doesn't even know it. He doesn't realize the impact he will soon have on people – a lot of people – all over the world. He isn't aware how his down-to-earth, humorous delivery and his courageous willingness to expose his soul will inspire so many people. He doesn't realize, yet, how he will encourage them to go beyond their limitations; perhaps even take advantage of those "limitations" to enhance their personal power and change their own corner of their world.

How? Serve – as he serves Lee at Broken Arrow. Focus on the simple things you can do right now. Keep your mind's eye on the big picture. Stay in touch with your customers. Listen, serve, take care of the details that help your businesses survive and succeed.

Chad has always been one to do whatever it is that needs doing. While he was in high school, his baseball team held a fundraising competition. A special, top of the line, bat was the grand prize. The distance a player could hit the ball, combined with the number of chocolate bars he sold, would determine the winner.

Chad was a good baseball player, but not the best batter. He really wanted that bat – I mean really, really, really! So he did what he had to do. His dad and I would taxi him and cases of candy bars all over the county. We'd drop him off with a couple boxes in a large housing division, then go back a few hours later and pick him up – minus the candy bars.

Maybe he couldn't hit the ball as well as some of the other boys, but he could hit every door everywhere. He could walk and knock. That, he could do and that, he did. *He did what others were not willing to do.*

He outsold his fellow teammates by a significant margin and, when the day came for the batting contest, he hit the ball... Well, he hit it as far as he could. It wasn't the farthest, but when his hit was combined with his sales, Chad walked away with his bat. He did it. He got it done. It is still the way he does business today.

How could his friends, his neighbors, his family know or even suspect that Chad will become, according to the Wall Street Journal, one of the ten most inspirational speakers in the world? How could they know that he will be one of the youngest and newest speakers ever to receive the Certified Speaking Professional distinction from National Speakers Association, be appointed to the NSA National Board, and honored in the National Speakers Hall of Fame?

On the other hand, those of us who really know Chad are not surprised by his success as a speaker. It isn't just the way he speaks; it's his constancy in taking care of business. It's his daily doing that get's things done. It may be subtle, but it's thematic in his message to Corporate America. *"Do"* is the operational word in *"DOne."*

For a long time I believed that Chad's accident was a tragedy. I was wrong. What seemed a tragedy has redefined itself as a gift. Actually, it didn't redefine itself. Chad's attitude and approach have redefined it.

I never would have imagined that I would say this, but the fact is that accident *was* a gift – a gift wrapped in ribbons of barbed wire – but a gift, nevertheless.

Ask Chad if he would change what happened. Ask him if he would choose not to have had the paralyzing accident. He says, "No." He doesn't just blurt it out, though. He pauses before he responds, weighing what he has lost against what he has gained. He is still my little baseball player. He yearns to feel the weight of a bat, to hear the crack of a hard-pitched ball smacked out of the park, and feel the wind in his hair as he sprints toward first base. On the other hand, he is deeply grateful for the opportunity to help businesses and individuals deal with their own personal trials and paralysis and disabilities.

Chad continues thoughtfully, "No, I wouldn't change what happened. That doesn't mean I don't wish to walk. It means I wouldn't sacrifice the friendships I have made, the people I've come to know and the opportunity I have to speak around the globe. I wouldn't change that. When I walk again, it will be according to God's plan and in God's time. It may be in this life or the next. For now, I am grateful for what I get to do. I get to make a difference."

"Courage is resistance to fear, mastery of fear
– not absence of fear.
Except a creature be part coward,
it is not a compliment to say it is brave!"

~ Mark Twain

Six

A Miracle Rolls In

This is not real. This can't be real.

I am a head, locked in a brace, bolted to the wall. My head is held motionless, and nothing else has the power to move. I have no body – no arms, no legs – at least, nothing I can sense.

My head is all that I am and all that I have; and it is held captive in a device of torture – that non-angelic halo brace. I can't move a single part of what once was me.

What isn't paralyzed and numb radiates incessant pain. I didn't know there were so many kinds of pain – dull aches from not moving; sharp unrelenting pain from those four pointed screws piercing my skull, dull thumping headache pain; throbbing pain from where I attempted to chew a hole in my lip to breathe, deep, permeating nausea from shock and medication.

Boredom, futility, and hopelessness engulf me as I lie here staring at the stark white composite ceiling. I can no longer hope to accomplish the dreams that lent enthusiasm and energy to my life. Life is over, as I know it. I am convinced.

A little over a century ago, Nietzsche, a well-known German philosopher and philologist, said, "Convictions are more dangerous enemies of truth than lies."[2]

---

[2] Friedrich Wilhelm Nietzsche (October 15, 1844 - August 25, 1900) 19th-century German philosopher and classical philologist. He believed we must question all doctrines that drain life's expansive energies, however socially prevalent those views might be. (Source: Wikipedia)

He believed in the honest questioning of any belief that drains one of enthusiasm for life. Nietzsche is right. We should have the courage of our convictions; but also the courage to question our convictions, especially when those convictions lead us to dismay or despair. And I certainly am in dismay and despair as I think of all that I have lost.

As these thoughts darken my mood, in comes the cavalry to the rescue. I could almost hear bugles and pounding hooves.

It's Dad.

Dad has become my own personal, self-appointed motivational speaker. He begins with gentle enthusiasm, "Son, I know this seems impossible, but…"

I know he's trying to be helpful. I know he is coming from a place of love and he doesn't want me to give up on life. But what does he know? Was he ever paralyzed from his neck to his toes? What qualifies him to understand what I am going through?

Dad may not have been paralyzed, but something did happen that helps him understand. Three months before my accident, Dad and his wife Terrie were attending a national business convention in Dallas, Texas. The keynote speaker was introduced: Hall of Fame speaker, Art Berg, a C6-quadriplegic from Salt Lake City, Utah.

Dad sat spellbound as this amazing presenter talked about overcoming life's difficulties:

"Dreams are never destroyed by circumstance. They live or die in your heart. My dreams come true not in spite of my circumstance but because of it… For those of us in this life who are afraid to change, life will change for us. Then it is always a more painful experience… Dream new dreams or dream old dreams in new ways. Think new thoughts or think old thoughts in new ways… The miracles of our lives do not come about by grand events, but by the little things we have chosen to do… The biggest problems come about, because I avoid the little things too long… The difficult takes time; the impossible just takes a little longer."

Never in his life had Dad been as moved as he was by Art's

presentation. As soon as he returned home, he contacted his three sons and told us he had a wonderful video of an amazing presentation and we all needed to get together and watch it.

We never did.

Now, here I am, three months later, a quadriplegic, just like Art Berg, and here is my dad coming to my rescue.

Chad with his dad, Kelly

"Son, what if I told you that you could be happier, more productive, and more successful with no hands and no legs than you ever were with them?"

I give him a look of utter disbelief, manage to force a mumbled "grrrmph" past the breathing tube and close my eyes stubbornly.

For a long moment, my dad looks at me with a mixture of understanding and disappointment. Then, without another word, he simply turns and walks away. He doesn't see a hurt kid. He sees an adult who isn't willing to be taught or willing to challenge his own despairing beliefs and conviction that all is lost.

I "grrrmph" again only in a different tone, desperately, with open and pleading eyes. This time "grrrmph" means, "Wait, don't leave. Dad, please don't leave." I begin to cry. I am a twenty-seven-year-old adult, married and a father of two children; but right now, I am the child and I need my dad. Like a child cries in the middle of the night, I cry for Dad to not leave me alone with this nightmare. I'll listen to his motivational speech if I have to. I really need him with me.

He pauses at the door. Turns. Dead serious. "Will you listen to what I have to say? Will you really listen to me, Son?"

Dad has just asked me if I could believe that I could be happier in a broken body than I ever was when I was whole. I am not buying it, but I don't want him to leave. After all, what else could he say that could be more unbelievable than saying I can be happier and more successful in this wreck of a body? That is just plain stupid. But I don't want to be alone, so I manage to push a halfhearted, "sure" past the breathing tube.

Dad comes back. He slides a videotape into the hospital room VCR. It is Art Berg's signature speech, "The Impossible Just Takes a Little Longer."

"Son, watch this."

I watch the tape without protest. What else am I going to do? I can't even turn my head.

When the speech is over, I don't remember one thing Art said. I do now; because I've watched it since – many times – and I still watch it every so often to remind myself of how possible impossible is. But I didn't really hear it then.

What I did notice was Art's body movement. How he contorted his body in order to move. Kind of a stretching, twisting movement he did occasionally as he spoke. I didn't understand it then. I understand it now.

I also notice his hands – when he gestures. His hands look like – well, they look like mine do now. Our hands are the same. Our bodies are the same. There is one thing we did not share, however. Art Berg is smiling. I am not. He laughs. I can't. The guy is happy. I am not. I sure do notice that!

A few weeks later, my hospital room door suddenly bumps open and in rolls Art Berg. He is in a manual – not electric – wheelchair. I recognize him from the video. He looks like me. His hands are clenched, his fingers curled into his palms. He has minimal movement in his torso. His legs don't move at all.

He doesn't say his name. He doesn't say "Hi, Chad." He doesn't say anything. He just wheels over to my bed, picks himself up out of his chair, and throws himself onto my bed.

Can you believe that? He lifts himself up out of his wheelchair and flops over onto my bed – without help! I had no idea that anyone in my circumstance could transfer, unaided, from chair to bed or from anywhere to anywhere, for that matter. How does he do that?

This guy's a quadriplegic. He has no stomach muscles, no chest muscles – none that work. No usable hands or forearms. He just pushes himself up. How?

I manage a surprised, "Hello?"

He doesn't reply, except to grin. Then he starts taking off his clothes.

He has my attention.

Art takes off his shirt without the use of his fingers. He undoes his belt with a little invention he made with wire. He removes his jeans. *Then he puts it all back on* – essentially with no workable hands or fingers – and arms that are 90% paralyzed.

Now he really has my attention.

After his little strip tease show, Art transfers back to his wheelchair, fishes around in a bag and pulls out a copy of his book, "Some Miracles Just Take a Little Longer." He signs it and hands it to me. He just did that with paralyzed hands and fingers. How?

What a demonstration! He isn't getting paid for this life-altering performance. He does it out of the goodness of his heart. He is teaching me. He is inspiring me. He is giving me confidence and hope – off the speaker's platform. He is challenging me to challenge my own beliefs – particularly my conviction that my life is over.

Maybe that's what great speakers and authors do best; inspire others to challenge their limiting beliefs; give them confidence and hope; and do it all the time, not just while on stage or in the pages of our books. Every waking, breathing moment we should live our message. It is important to walk our talk, so to speak, and whenever we speak, speak encouragement and hope. It helps *us,* too. What we do off the platform gives us greater presence and authenticity while we're on it.

At this time, however, I don't really make the connection that Art is a speaker. I just see a happy, paralyzed guy giving an unhappy paralyzed guy the greatest gift of all – hope. Not by preaching, but simply by *doing*. Doing what? Doing simple things that are no longer simple for me – things I consider outside my range of possibility.

Art Berg

For the next nine months, I stay in close contact with him. I learn from him, am inspired and encouraged by him. I am always bugging someone to help me email him with all kinds of questions. He answers every email.

We have interesting parallels. Like me, Art is the father of two children, and husband to a beautiful woman. Like me, he became paralyzed just when his life was going really great. Like me, he is struck down in his prime. But rather than stay down, which no one would have blamed him for, he moves forward.

Now, Art has a wonderful career traveling the world, speaking to civic groups, schools and churches, small businesses, professional associations, hospitals, medical and huge corporate conventions.

Could I be like him? Can I move like him? Can I move *forward* like him? Can I be a good husband and father? Can I have a rewarding career? Can I have any kind of career? Everyone needs someone to look up to, someone to guide them, especially through difficult times when our business or personal life takes an unexpected turn.

Mine has sure taken a turn – upside-down!

Art helps me turn it right side up again.

Family, friends, therapists and doctors do wonders for me. However, Art does something no one else can do. He lets me look deep into his personal world – his quadriplegic world. This man is president-elect of the National Speakers Association, an NSA Hall of Fame speaking professional with a thriving business that keeps him traveling thousands of miles a year, speaking to audiences all around the globe. Yet here he is, focusing time and attention on me; someone he didn't even know until the day he rolled into my hospital room.

He brings me into his home and into his life. He lets me watch him operate his business, do housework like a real man, and, most importantly, he lets me watch as he takes care of his personal needs like shaving, dressing, brushing his teeth, etc.

Sharing the "etc" – the really personal stuff – is incredibly helpful and encouraging. I begin to understand on a very real level that I can be "normal," as long as I have the strength to challenge my convictions, and am willing to be "normal" differently.

Art isn't just a business and family man. He is an athlete. Truly. He plays full contact wheelchair rugby. These gutsy athletes don't let their disabilities stop them from competing. They throw themselves around with reckless abandon in wheelchairs that closely resemble demolition-derby cars. The Denver Harlequins, a quadriplegic rugby team, has an interesting motto: "It ain't real, if it don't bend steel!"

Competition? Hmmm… can I do that?

How about Art's 1993 marathon? Ten years after an auto accident costs him the use of his legs and severely limits the use of his arms and hands, Art pedals his hand-operated tri-wheel wheelchair from Salt Lake City to St. George, Utah, setting a three hundred and thirty-five-mile world record. This guy is "wheelin' and dealin'" with life better than most "able bodied" people I know.

Hmmm… a marathon. Could I do something like that?

I pay little attention to his speaking business. I don't see myself as a speaker, and running a business of any kind seems way beyond me. But these other things he was doing catch my attention. If he can do such things… well… I don't know that I can do all that… But maybe… I have to try something. Anything to get out of the house.

Family life now revolves around taking care of me. This is not acceptable. I need to take care of them. Shondell and our boys need a sense of normalcy and so do I. I am ready to move forward. I have to do something, somehow. I don't exactly know what I will do or how, but I need to get out of the house. I need to go to work and "bring home the bacon." I feel like *The Little Engine That Could:* "I think I can, I think I can." But I also feel derailed. Where do I go? How can I work? What can I do?

It is as though this whirlwind of thoughts creates a vortex that begins to draw in possibilities. My friend Lee Johnson steps in.

Lee and his wife Cathy have been close friends of ours for years. Lee is the general manager of Broken Arrow, a construction company. He asks me to help him out at his company – maybe do some clerical work or something. At this time, I can barely pick up a pencil, much less write anything with it; however, I agree to give it a shot. I don't know how I am going to do it, but Art Berg has inspired me to believe that anything is possible.

Lee's offer is hard to accept, though. Lee doesn't act like he is doing me a favor, but it still feels like charity. His kind offer feels like just that – kindness. How could he possibly think I would be of any real help in a construction company? That's a world of trucks, lumber, cement, tool belts, muscle and sweat. How on earth could a quadriplegic fit in that kind of world with that kind of energy? I have no idea.

This is one of my toughest life lessons – to learn to accept the kindness and generosity of others and move ahead with faith. I keep my doubts to myself. I swallow my pride– and humbly accept his offer.

I start immediately. Five days a week, Cathy picks me up for work. She helps Shondell transfer me to her car and then she drives me to the job site. When we arrive, Lee helps transfer me from the car to my chair and I push my way up the ramp he built for me to get into his office where I start work. When I say I start work in "his office," I mean it literally

Lee is the head honcho, so he has the best office. It's right in front. I can't get up the stairs where the other office workers are, so Lee gives me his big beautiful office. I am flabbergasted. Talk about reasonable accommodation! He has no guarantees of what I can do, but he gives me a chance – and his office!

If I wasn't humbled before, I sure am now.

Here in my own private haven, I reacquaint myself with the world of business. I don't have much physical ability or strength. Even simple office tasks can be nearly impossible for a new quadriplegic. But I hear Art Berg's voice in my head. "Chad, you and I can do anything anyone else can, if we are willing to do it differently." I hear my dad's voice saying, "Amen!"

There are so many things I cannot do. If I tried to write them all down, the list would stretch into next Thursday. But what if I shifted my focus? What if I focused on what I *can* do instead of what I *can't,* I start listing what I have left rather than what I have lost. I come to realize that is a pretty big list, too. Family, friends, faith…

One thing I do have left is my voice – and it is getting stronger all the time.

Lee and I get together and make a plan. We focus on what I can do. I can handle the phones and a computer. With a little adaptive equipment – like the special gloves developed by my friends at rehab – I can dial the phone and handle a computer keyboard. I use a headset, so I don't have to use the speakerphone and sound like I am calling from a cave. This is my first job. Answering phones. Taking messages. I am a receptionist.

Like riding a bike, takin' care of business comes back to me fast. I begin by focusing on simple clerical tasks at hand. I keep in touch with customers. I learn to listen. Serve. Take care of daily details. My responsibilities are fundamental, my contributions simple. I arrive at work on time and with the right attitude. Anyone can do that. Not everyone does. Every day, I do all the little things that help businesses large or small survive and then succeed. Because of Lee and Cathy's faith in me, and their willingness to give me an opportunity, a transformation takes place almost instantly. I am a breadwinner again.

Maybe Lee is not an expert on hiring the handicapped and accommodation and all that, but Lee saw something in me that I think a lot of businessmen fail to see in the disabled.

He saw me.

He saw Chad.

He didn't see a broken fellow in a wheelchair. He saw someone with something to contribute, even though, at first, he didn't know what I could contribute. At Broken Arrow, I didn't feel broken. I didn't feel different. I felt like a member of a team. I responded accordingly. I used every bit of the drive and focus I used in building my own business and running my ranch into serving my friend. I do things. I get things *DOne*.

Sometimes, if you really pay attention to who you are hiring – the *person* you are hiring – and accommodate their difficulties, and do so not out of pity but because you respect what they have to offer, such as the perseverance and creativity they have developed while dealing successfully with their difficulties, you give yourself the gift.

Opportunity was Lee's gift to me.

Dedication, focus, and loyalty were my gifts to Lee.

At Broken Arrow, I rediscover something I thought I had lost; something vital for my future – and the future of my family – my confidence and my ability to run a business. Because of Lee's faith in me, I reinvent myself as a contributing human being and a working professional. I am a husband and father, providing financially for my family.

I develop great relationships with Lee's regular customers and start to get outstanding bills collected. I don't see myself as a collector; I am just developing relationships and getting people to honor their commitments. I surprise Lee, and myself, by bringing in a fifteen thousand dollar debt that had gone uncollected for several years. Lee turns collections over to me entirely and also puts me in charge of sales.

Every time I give more, I gain more. I already have Lee's office; now I get my own secretary!

Then something happens that gives me new direction and purpose. Lee asks me to speak at our Christmas luncheon at Broken Arrow. I didn't know what to say, so I simply told my story. I guess they like my stories, because the CEO heard me speak and asked me to speak to all five hundred employees. He assigned me to speak about taking initiative, dealing with challenges, and doing all you can with all you have. I spoke to forty employees at a time at intimate luncheon meetings every Wednesday. It was fun. It was challenging. It started me thinking.

Small opportunities can lead to big things, if we are willing to do the little things that are needed to get big things *DOne*. With a lot faith from my employer, and a little adaptive equipment – I return to the land of the living. Because of my employer's faith in me, I am again the breadwinner – and a husband and father again. Now I understand my dad's challenge. I *can* be happier, more productive, and more successful than ever before. I can run a successful business. I can be a husband and father. I may have to do everything differently, but I can do everything – and get it *DOne*.

Several months later, I am asked to speak a similar message of encouragement at a church meeting. Afterwards, a member of the congregation asks me how much I would charge to bring his employees the same message. I have no idea. I never really saw myself as a speaker. Can I do it? Could I even become a professional like Art?

I begin to dream again.

I call my mentor. He insists that I can do this – and do it well. He takes me with him to speaking engagements. He shows me how to better connect with my audiences. He shows me how to get real and communicate from the heart. He brings me into his office and teaches me how to build and manage my own speaking business.

Art Berg, mentor to millions, became my personal mentor and still is – from the other side. February 12, 2002, five days after returning from a trip to Hawaii with Shondell and me, Art Berg, age 39, dies unexpectedly in his sleep.

I am stunned. Art has given me hope and inspiration. He has been my anchor and the wind in my sails. Now, this incredible man – this man who blew into my life like a summer storm is – just as suddenly – gone.

At Art's funeral, I sit quietly amidst the slow swirl of mourners. I wonder why so many precious things are taken from us just when we appreciate them the most.

"The Lord giveth and the Lord taketh away…" This just doesn't make sense.

Yet.

Chad with Art Berg

Accept responsibility, regardless of fault.
Then *DO* what needs to be *DOne*.

This is your key to survival and success.

~ *Chad Hymas*

Seven

Response-ability

Let's go back in time to my hospital room a few weeks before Art Berg rolls into my life.

A family member is always close by as I move gingerly through the valley of life and death. They eventually work out a schedule to spell each other. But these first three days, almost everyone is at the hospital with me – and I need every one of them here.

At the hospital, at church, at home, countless prayers are offered. My Catholic mother lights candles and goes to Mass. My Mormon dad gives me blessings and places my name on the Temple prayer roll. The rest of my family and friends add their prayers to Mom's and Dad's, asking – no, fervently pleading – for a better outcome than the one the doctors have predicted.

Days pass with little change. A friend of my mother's, a Jehovah's Witness, calls Mom, "Laureen, do you mind if we put Chad's name on *our* prayer list? You Catholics and Mormons just aren't getting the job done!"

Trying to breathe in my condition is like deep sea diving with a leaky air hose. Then insult is added to injury. They reverse the process, so they can vacuum out mucus from my lungs. They use a forced water vacuum system – sort of like the one used to clean your carpets.

The nurse pushes a water tube inside the breathing tube that is already in place. Without resistance, it slides down my throat and into a lung. The nurse turns on what feels like a fire hydrant and floods that lung with warm sterile water. She then reverses the process and sucks out the water along with all the junk that has collected in there over the last few hours. My eyes beg for mercy – to no avail. As I contemplate all my past sins in preparation for sure death from drowning, she floods the other lung.

Every three hours, I drown – literally, horribly, drown. Can you imagine a couple of gallons of water being poured into your lungs? It exceeds your worst nightmare. Repeated four to eight times a day, this procedure is as necessary as it is miserable. The pain and panic of drowning is not reduced by my numbness and paralysis. I feel every bit of it. I am positive I am going to die. I really would die if it took any longer than it does. I believe it. My body *knows* it.

My brother Brian is in the room one afternoon when the nurse instigates this procedure. As she floods the first lung, my body suddenly convulses and goes into involuntary spasms. It is exceptionally painful, even today, when these spasms happen. It is actually more like pressure – huge pressure – a monstrous vice clamping down on my chest. I can't breathe. I can't think. My body becomes an alien creature out of control.

After the procedure, I am traumatized, in residual pain and panic – harboring real fear for the next time this will happen – which will be in another three hours. Brian is as traumatized as I am – maybe more so. Witnessing a loved one's pain is usually far more difficult than dealing with your own.

The procedure lasts less than a minute, but it is pure Hell.

Hell is sometimes essential to healing.

Brian goes to the nurses' station and pleads with them to give me something to relieve my agony and panic. They gently explain to him that, although this procedure is an awful experience, it is too dangerous to drug me. I am barely alive, and they can't risk taking me down any further. I am near the bottom already, and at the *very* bottom lies death.

Brian returns to my room, lays his head on my shoulder and weeps. If I could stroke my brother's head or pat his arm to show how much I appreciate his being there for me, I would. My brother's love and compassion calm me more than any medication could.

Nights are the worst. I sleep fitfully. I am filled with unnamed fears; afraid to let myself slide into real sleep; afraid of the shadows that seem to move just out of my range of vision; afraid that they will materialize into deadly phantoms; afraid of weird hospital sounds that go "bump" "whoosh" and "sigh" in the night.

I am afraid of my nightmares, but I am even more afraid of my good dreams. I dream of pleasant hours with Shondell; playing in the sun with my boys; working on my beautiful elk ranch. It tears my soul to leave these sweet dreams and awaken to the nightmare that is my new reality.

I lie alone in the dark, staring wide-eyed at the ceiling. What if something happens – real or imagined? What if I choke or a slimy green monster crawls out from under the bed to kill me? I will surely die a horrible death, because my numb fingers can't push the call button.

The nurses fasten the emergency call button to my gown with a safety pin so I can press it with my chin; but it slips down out of reach and I am left to lie there – and die there. My fears are real. At least they are to me. I wish you could understand how totally helpless and scared I am. Why? *So you will understand that experiencing this condition of total helplessness reveals the key to my survival and eventual success.*

My family responds as a cohesive unit to my need for protection from these daunting nightmares – both imagined and real. They never leave me by myself. My brother, Brian, and Shondell's sister, Alisa, are my night-shift tag-team. They alternate evenings, sleeping in a chair in my hospital room.

Shondell's sister, Alisa, is eighteen years old and much like Shondell in looks and personality. She is at the age when most girls are focused on boys, school, boys, music, boys, friends, boys and boys. But she gives up her social life to spend her evenings with her broken, paranoid, brother-in-law. When Shondell, Mom, or my brothers aren't here, Alisa becomes my personal angel.

I'll walk again. I believe that. It hasn't really hit me how much damage has been done. My mood slowly begins to shift. I become increasingly hopeful and positive; at least when it is daylight and the green, slimy monsters under my bed are asleep. The doctors decide a mental health therapist isn't necessary. I haven't told them about the green monsters. I am fine emotionally – really. I can – and will – overcome any obstacle, challenge or problem. Nothing will keep me from living a full and successful life.

I interpret living a "full and successful life" as most people do. I define it as being healed and "able-bodied" again. I mean, after all, how could anyone accept this condition? And why would they? Why should they? They shouldn't! That wouldn't be "positive" would it? That would be giving up and giving in, right? I intend to be healed. I will be healed. I have decided. That's that.

In the meantime, I lie here, trying to absorb the doctors' message that I am helpless and hopeless. The list of the things I can do is very short. The list of things I can't do is very long.

At the top of my "Can't do" list is breathe on my own. I must learn how to do that or I'll be stuck in this place for the rest of my life with breathing tube down my throat. That is not acceptable.

I begin my long road back. One step at a time. Doing what can be done.

Step one? Learn to breathe on my own. That is no small feat. My diaphragm is my only working chest muscle. It must learn how to compensate for the loss of the other three.

I practice on a small respirator tube designed to see how many little white plastic balls I can keep in the air for twenty seconds. I am to start with ten seconds, then eventually move up to enough 'oomph' to keep those little balls suspended for twenty seconds.

Doctors, nurses and therapists have other patients. Other than an occasional encouraging word and pat on the back, they no longer have time to coach me. So my regular coach starts in again. Dad wants me free of this hated breathing tube as much as I do.

Shondell helps, too. Mom hardly ever leaves my side except to care for our boys so Shondell can be here as much as possible.

They disconnect the breathing apparatus, and I gasp like a trout out of water for as long as I can before they have to reconnect me. Shondell keeps track of the time. I rest for five minutes, and then try again, hoping to beat my previous record. I spend hours at this.

Seven days later, I can breathe on my own – for three hours at a time. Three hours! It is like coming over the top of a series of ice bound mountain ranges and suddenly seeing a green valley stretched out before you. At the other end of the valley is home.

I miss my boys. If anything can make me feel better about my circumstance and give me the energy and focus I need to survive and eventually get home, it is the thought of seeing my children again and feeling that I'm still their daddy.

I ask to see my boys.

The doctor says, "No."

He says there are two good reasons why not.

First, it is against hospital policy for anyone under the age of eight to enter the intensive care unit. The second reason is that I still look like something from outer space. The breathing tube has been removed, but I still have those hateful sensor wires, feeding tubes and the like – all over the place. Dad says I resemble the distributor cap from Mom's '68 Camaro's V8 engine.

The doctor is right. I want to see my children, but I do not want *them* to see *me* – not like this. There is a simple solution, right? Yes, there is.

"Well, then, let's get this stuff off me." My enthusiasm sometimes exceeds my reason.

He smiles patiently, and shakes his head.

I become a motivational speaker for the first time in my life. The only thing that works is my mouth – and I work it! Finally, in utter exhaustion, I suppose, and the need to see his other fifty patients sometime before midnight, the doctor cuts me a deal.

"Okay, Chad, show me you can drink two thousand CCs of water a day without drowning and eat twelve hundred calories worth of real food without choking. Learn to do these two simple things and I will remove the rest of the tubes and wires so you can see your kids without scaring the bejabbers out of them."

Ah. Simple, doable goals, right? Not exactly. It's a tall order. It is simple, but it is not easy, not by a long shot. Can you imagine a job description that reads like this: "Must have the ability to drink without drowning; must be skilled at eating a chicken leg without dying?"

Well, that is now my job description. My performance plan. Payday will be when I get the job done. My paycheck? Getting to see my kids again – and oh, how I miss them.

This will be no walk in the park. Like learning to breathe on my own, it requires incredible effort and focus to develop the two simple skills of eating and drinking. Yes, for those of you who breathe, chew and swallow without thinking (or choking), they are skills – very exacting skills, in fact – but I know I can do it. I have already gotten rid of the dreaded breathing tube. This I can do too.

The main goal is getting a significant percentage of my meal into my mouth – that's step one. Then I get to swallow it. That's a whole different deal.

I fail the liquid swallow test three times before I master getting fluid down to my stomach, rather than into my lungs. In this test and the solid food test, the motivation is twofold: Get it right, I go home to the ranch. Get it wrong, I go home to the big mansion in the sky. I am excited. I will risk the mansion in the sky for one bite of real food and the chance to go home.

They come in with the solid food test. I am excited! My first real meal since the accident! I am salivating. I can't wait. What will it be? Steak? Heck, I'll settle for Campbell's chicken soup – or just the crackers!

The first course?

Ice chips.

I manage to chew an ice chip.

Sigh.

After they leave, I get to thinking. Ice? How about some flavor? A little fruit flavoring can't hurt. I beg my sister-in-law, Jennilyn, to smuggle in a cherry Popsicle.

This is my second presentation as a motivational speaker. I have an audience of one. I plead with her, "Please, just a popsicle. What can that hurt?" I reason with her, "They let me eat ice, why not a little flavoring in the ice?" I am as convincing and conniving as I am desperate. Food, real food, is the goal and I am not giving up. She leaves on her nefarious mission, and soon returns with the contraband.

They catch her at the door.

The doctors take her aside and somberly explain what could happen if I get food in my lungs. Pneumonia. Death. I am not allowed solid food. I won't be for weeks.

Eating is a skill. Watch a two-year-old in his high chair decorate his face with spaghetti. You get the idea.

I graduate from ice chips to Jell-O, anything thin enough to go down easily, but thick enough to make it past the lungs. It is surprisingly difficult to learn how to eat and drink; to learn how to get food down the right pipe without choking.

Shondell keeps track of my successes on a chart on a clipboard. I think she enjoys this. I am surprised she doesn't wear a white lab coat. "First, you take a drink. Just a little. Now swallow it. Good. Now take a bite. It helps if you get most of it into your mouth. Yes. Now swallow. No choking…"

In baby steps, incrementally, I gain the life skills of a two-year-old.

I drink the required two thousand CC's and eat the required twelve hundred calories. I pass both tests on the twelfth day. It is seven or eight o'clock on Sunday evening. Shondell helps me add up what we've accomplished.

I can breathe.

I can eat.

Air goes into my lungs.

Food and water go into my stomach.

I have completed the assigned tasks at the required level of competence.

Excellent!

Time to call the doctor.

Shondell takes her report to the head nurse on duty. "We want the doctor's home phone number, please," she asks charmingly.

It is Sunday evening. The doctor is probably with his family. I understand. I have a family, too. But I want to see my pal Christian and I haven't seen little Kyler walk, yet. I know I should be more patient, but my need to see my boys is overwhelming.

Shondell comes back to my room with a triumphant smile on her face, dials the doctor's home number, and holds the phone to my ear.

"I've done everything I am supposed to do," I declare firmly. "I haven't seen my kids for two weeks. I want to see them – tonight."

My voice softens despite my effort to stay tough. "Can you please come here and remove these tubes?"

Dr. Ryser is wonderful. He is at the hospital in fifteen minutes and removes all the tubes.

Shondell leaves while the staff transfers me to my new room in the rehab unit.

At 9:30 that evening, Shondell returns with my boys. One-year-old Kyler toddles to my bedside, looks up quizzically, then hurries back to Mommy's arms.

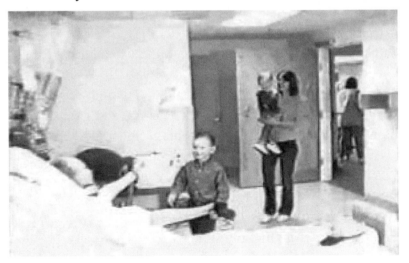

Shondell, Christian and Kyler coming to see Chad

Christian runs over and jumps up on the bed. He gives me a big hug, and then looks me over curiously, "Dad, why are you wearing diapers?"

I haven't really thought of this, but sure enough, I am wearing a diaper. How do I explain this to my little boy?

"Christian, I have to wear one of these for a while, I guess."

He gets it. He understands. I don't know how, but he does. "That's okay, Dad. You can practice on Kyler's potty chair."

It is amazing how my young son adapts so quickly to circumstances that would be daunting to an adult. Why can't we – adults and employers – be as accepting of others' differences and different circumstances? I guess we can, if we think about it.

Maybe that's partly why I am writing this book.

By the way, I want you to know that I did practice and now I no longer wear diapers.

My family spends that night with me. Christian sleeps on the bed next to me. Kyler sleeps with his mother on a cot just a few feet away. The next morning, I awaken to Christian's urgent nudging.

"What's wrong?" I ask.

"I had bad dreams 'bout the helicopter that flew you away. I wet the bed, Dad."

Christian hasn't had an accident in over a year.

"That's okay, Christian. Hop off the bed, run over to the bathroom and get yourself cleaned up. Mom's still asleep. It will be our little secret."

No sooner does he climb off the bed, than the nurse walks in. Christian, ashamed of his wet pajamas, skids to a halt, slams it in reverse, and jumps back in bed. He pulls the sheet over his face, and pretends he is still asleep.

The nurse isn't fooled, but plays along.

"Christian! Time to wake up. I need your help. We're going to teach Daddy how to eat breakfast by himself."

Christian doesn't move. "I'll have my breakfast in bed."

I have taught my son well.

"No," says the nurse. "You can't have breakfast in bed. We need to take your father to the cafeteria where they have special utensils he can eat with."

Christian doesn't budge.

"Christian," she says firmly, "I need to get Daddy ready. I will do it with you or without you, but I could really use your help."

My son thinks for a moment; then answers, "Okay, I'll help. But Daddy wet the bed last night."

I can't believe what I am hearing! My son is blaming me. What is our relationship coming to?

The nurse checks out the situation. "Christian, your father's not wet. He's dry."

Christian thinks for a moment then stoutly declares, "I know. That's 'cause he got it all over me."

He soon redeems himself. I am helpless – but not without help. My little boy, with a little help from the nurse, takes off my bedclothes. With a big-kid smile on his face, he helps put on my shirt, pants, socks, and shoes.

Then, without anyone's help, my son combs my hair and brushes my teeth (and my nose). After Shondell shaves me, Christian pats my cheeks with cologne. Old Spice is his favorite, because he likes the picture of the boat on the bottle.

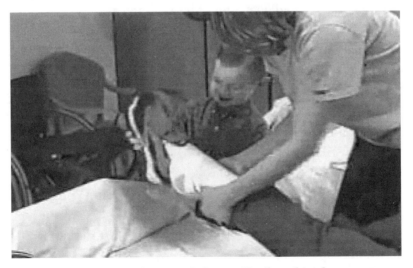

Shondell and Christian helping Chad get his shoes on

This is a tender moment. It brings tears to my eyes. In a matter of seconds, this child acknowledges, accepts, adapts, and acts on a new situation. Adults should have such flexibility. Acknowledge... Accept... Adapt... Act... a simple, but powerful process for dealing with change. Big events – death, lost relationships, lost opportunities, changing financial circumstances – often throw us grown-ups for a loop – even into a state of paralysis. Kids seem to be able to adapt almost instantly. They can change in a blink, without going through the why-ner stage my friend Kevin Hall refers to in his book "Aspire." Visit the Shriners' Hospital in your area and you'll see what I mean.

I'm thankful for what my son just taught me. Christian's acceptance of his Dad's new circumstances shifts my thinking. My approach to seemingly insurmountable problems and challenges is changed forever.

I am proud of my little boy's acceptance of other's situations, but I keep thinking about his refusal to accept his own responsibility. Why did he refuse to admit wetting the bed?

A 200-watt bulb switches on.

He learned it from me.

I'm not taking responsibility for my life. I'm blaming everyone and everything for my accident and my paralysis. Why? It's necessary for my psychological and emotional survival to blame someone else – anyone else – for what happened. Isn't it? Some burdens are too heavy to bear alone. If I take the blame for my own lack of common sense – taking seven minutes to add hydraulic fluid to my tractor's reservoir – a simple act that would have prevented the accident and this unbelievable personal and family devastation, I will sink into a place so dark and deep I don't know how I could ever climb out of it.

So, I must blame everyone else.

The doctors waited over two hours to get the steroids into my neck after I arrived at the hospital. Time is everything when you have a spinal cord injury.3 If the procedure had happened sooner, I might

---

3 The synthetic steroid methylprednisolone (MP) helps fight the inflammation that occurs with a spinal cord injury. Immediately following the trauma, the nervous system starts to fall

have bladder control or feeling in my toes or maybe a little more dexterity in my fingers. Why did it take them so long? I have no feeling in most of my body, no function in my legs, no bladder control, and no use of my fingers.

It is the doctors' fault.

Why did my wife wait so long before coming to look for me? It was 45 minutes before she found me. Why did it take her so long?

It is my wife's fault.

I blame that rotten piece of equipment, that old tractor.

It is Henry Fords' fault.

I blame the officer who didn't have the sense to cut the strings off the hay bale. It's so simple, so easy. Cut the strings.

It is the cop's fault!

The fact is that I have not cut the strings myself. I am not willing to let go of what might have been, and deal with what is.

When things go wrong, we tend to blame our problems on others or on circumstances beyond our control. This is a natural and very human tendency. Why do we do that? As I said earlier, if we blame ourselves, we may invite a level of regret that we are not ready to bear.

There's a simple solution. Get rid of blame and regret. Dump guilt and remorse. Instead of assigning blame and guilt to ourselves or anyone else, let's just accept responsibility. Response-ability. Our ability to respond to a situation regardless of whose "fault" it may be.

What about Christian and his childish excuses? How else could he come up with the idea of blaming someone else, if he wasn't trained to think that way? I'm the father. I'm the one who is supposed to teach my son by my example. Yet, now, our roles are reversed. He

---

apart, from the point of injury moving downward. The inflammation causes the breakdown of fats into free radicals that act like acid on the cell tissue. Healthy tissue below the injury site is destroyed. MP must be given within eight hours of the injury to have any effect and, in most patients, can reduce the problem by about 20%. This can mean the difference between bladder control or none, feeling in the legs, or none.

is showing me by *his* example that it doesn't matter why we are in the situation we are in, we just need to acknowledge our circumstances and accept our responsibility. Regardless of fault or blame, we need to move forward and do what needs to be *DO*ne. This is key to survival and success.

"Develop success from failures.
Discouragement and failure are two of the surest
stepping stones to success."

~ Dale Carnegie

Eight

Life Skills of a Two-Year-Old

Some rehab patients want to be left alone. Some accept the way they are. Some get discouraged and want to give up. Some do give up. Some respond to being pushed. Some don't. I am a mixture of all of the above. For the most part, I am enthused about the challenge of rehabilitation. I am ready to deal and heal.

I make up my mind to regain my freedom and independence one muscle at a time. I have faith that I can do this. I will add power to that faith by learning specific techniques. Rather than be frustrated with the exhausting difficulty of trying to move an unresponsive finger or toe, or revitalizing one additional chest muscle, I am determined to have fun doing it.

I must relearn how to hold a fork, brush my teeth, and shave. Before I can do any of these things, however, I have to learn how to sit up without passing out. That is my first and most difficult task. I know that some mornings this is *your* first and most difficult task, so you can relate!

My day begins as a rehab therapist raises my bed to a forty-five degree angle.

I pass out.

There goes the morning.

The next day we get to do it again.

The next day we do it again.

The next day… (sigh…)

As my upper body is raised to a position much higher than flat on my back, the blood rushes down to my toes, because the muscles governing the veins do not contract like they used to and help keep my blood moving in the right direction.

So, I pass out.

We do this fun exercise over and over again.

The bed is cranked up, putting me somewhere in the neighborhood of a sitting position and, whoosh, I'm gone.

At least, I get to make up for all that sleep I missed worrying about slimy green monsters hiding under my bed.

Next, I get to wear nylons.

These tight white nylons are called TED hose. Some even call them "support hose." They are designed to compress the veins and prevent blood from rushing to your legs and feet – taking with it your brain's oxygen supply… and your consciousness. These extremely tight stockings go from my toes to my thighs. It takes three nurses to get them on; but get them on, they do.

They crank up my bed again.

I pass out again.

So they tape my feet – tight.

I don't know how or why this is all supposed to work, but apparently, repeatedly telling my system to either work or go comatose teaches it – with no intellectual involvement on my part – to do what it's told. And it does – eventually.

Finally, I can sit up.

I can't sit up to a full 90-degree angle. Not yet. This will come in time. The tights and the taped feet allow me to be advanced to a 60- or 65-degree angle. I feel lightheaded, but I don't faint.

After a week of this, I finally achieve my goal. I have gained one of the life skills of a six-month-old infant. I can sit up on my own.

Sitting up is one thing. Staying up is another. Have you ever noticed how many muscles it takes to keep you upright? Dealing with profound paralysis means I have to learn how to sit up – and stay sitting up – differently than you do.

This is accomplished slowly. The learning process starts in rehab and continues when I go home. Shondell and Christian help me with daily balance practice. We make it fun. We set frustration aside. We focus on the challenge. My team gets fully involved, and we play.

Shondell sits behind me on the bed, helping me maintain equilibrium. Christian stands in front of me. Using my shoulder muscles, I raise my arms straight out to either side, like a circus performer balancing on a high wire.

Christian exclaims, "Look, Dad, you're flying."

My son's spontaneous and inspiring comment gives birth to my first business motto: "*Who needs legs when you have wings?*"

I can now sit up without toppling over like a felled oak. We start reducing the amount of tape on my feet and incrementally move the tights down to my knees, because my body is somehow starting to work better in this respect.

Finally, the tape and the compression stockings are discarded entirely. "One small step for a man, one giant leap..." Okay, just baby steps, for now.

Remember that strange stretching twisting movement Art Berg made when he was speaking? It is an essential survival skill for people confined to wheelchairs. It is important for those of us who are paralyzed to shift our weight while sitting or lying down. We must prevent pressure sores, usually referred to as bedsores. If we don't move regularly, the blood circulation is restricted from the part of the body that is bearing the weight. The skin dies a little. A sore forms. The sore gets infected and goes septic. It is often fatal.

When you sit, you can't sit perfectly still for long. Every once in a while, you shift your weight so you aren't compressing nerves and blood vessels. If you don't, your nether region goes numb. Numbness, tingling, or just some slight muscle ache or restlessness is a healthy, functioning body's way of getting you to move a little. Most of the time, you aren't even aware you are moving.

I don't feel that kind of discomfort anymore. My body doesn't tell me I've been sitting in the same position too long, cutting off circulation or compressing nerves. I have to remind myself to move, constantly shifting myself so that my blood vessels get oxygen where it is needed so I do not get an infection that can easily kill me.

Helping me in this process is the fact that I constantly feel some level of pain. Wait. Haven't I said that I can't feel anything from the shoulders down? Well, yes. I can't feel external touch or pressure, but damaged nerves are constantly reminding me that they are still alive. I get shocks or pings or waves of pain that tell me that my body is still there.

Christopher Reeve died of heart failure in October of 2004. Why? Because of pressure wounds that became septic. This infection caused heart failure. Christopher Reeve had the best medical care money can buy, yet his death was a common result of problems stemming from infection from a pressure wound.

Superman was not felled by kryptonite. He was killed by a bedsore.

I am told I would have to use an electric wheelchair for the rest of my life. That's okay. Electric wheelchairs are fun. It takes me three days to learn how to operate the controls with my chin and my wrists. It is worth it. Mastering the electric wheelchair makes me incredibly happy. Strapped in like a demolition derby driver, I fling about at a mad pace approaching the speed of light. I travel to different floors. I go outside in the sunshine and fresh air. Bouncing over speed bumps, plowing through grass and gravel, I am free. Free to roam on my own.

My joy is short-lived.

Shondell comes to visit. I can tell by her face that something is up. The doctors asked her to convince me to try a manual wheelchair. I don't think Shondell and I ever had a bigger argument. This motorized wheel chair has given me my first taste of freedom. I will not give that up. I respond with an emphatic, "No. That's final!"

"Final" is a word I will never use again in an argument with my sweet, but determined wife.

"Look, Shondell, look what I can do with my electric wheelchair. See how I can maneuver this thing? It's great. Why take that away from me? How can I use a manual chair? I have no grip. I have no feeling in my arms. How can I push it? The doctors said I have to use an electric wheelchair. Have they forgotten?"

"Chad, they'll teach you. They think you can develop the muscles in your arms."

This only adds to my frustration. It is humiliating to remind your beautiful, sexy wife how broken you are. "Shondell, you can't develop what you don't have."

I am completely numb to my fingertips. The only really usable muscles in my arms are my biceps. The doctors know this. They want me to use them and keep them strong. Using a manual wheelchair will help.

I don't care. Life is hard enough. Why try something so unnecessarily difficult? I just learned to use the power chair. It's fun. I like how things are. I have freedom and I love it. Doesn't anyone understand that?

I can't walk, but I can dig in my heels. Again, I flatly refuse. "No. I'm not going to do that."

My resolve lasts only a short time. You don't hold out against Shondell. Not when she is determined.

The next morning, she won't help me out of bed, won't help me dress – not until I decide to give the manual wheelchair a try. Shondell is relentless. She really isn't bossy or controlling, but the doctors have convinced her that I should try, so she holds firm.

She is tough when she knows what is best.

I give in.

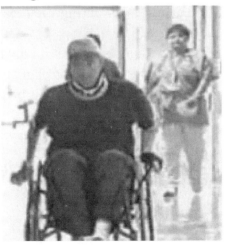

Chad learning to use the manual wheelchair

The first time I attempt to push forward in the manual chair, my numb, dysfunctional hands slip off the wheel rings and I fall out of the chair. My head hits the floor. I am not amused. The therapists are not sympathetic. Do they care? Do they say, "That's okay. You tried. Let's help you back into your power chair so life can be easier."

Nope. They just put different wheels on the manual chair and plunk me right back in it. The new wheels have foam covered pegs coming out the sides, much like the deadly spokes in the chariots in the grand arena in the movie "Gladiator." They are spaced six inches apart so I have something for my numb hands to push against.

"Try for ten yards," the therapist says.

Ten yards? That's about the same as ten miles to everyone else. I look up. Shondell is standing there with that look on her face.

I sigh.

I push.

I push again – and again – but I don't even get past one floor tile. I am pooped. I am angry. I want more freedom. But at this cost?

I'm not sure it's worth it, but I keep trying. I learn how to apply pressure with my wrists. I push with them, even though I can't feel them. Eventually, I make my ten-yard goal. I pay the price and get it *DOne,* one inch at a time, one floor tile at a time. It is worth it. By the time I leave the hospital, I can wheel down the corridors without the special pegs. In the future, I rarely use an electric wheelchair, except to negotiate soft ground as when I cheer my boys during their ball games or coach a soccer team.

Freedom isn't free. We believe freedom is our right, but it comes with a price. We may have to deal with despair, and endure pain and frustration. Sometimes we can only move toward freedom, one inch, one foot, one yard at a time.

Slowly, I regain the life skills of a two-year-old. Day after day, I do what needs to be *DOne* in order to be free.

Don't give in to your deprivations.
Live up to your expectations.

~ Chad Hymas

Nine

Wheelin' & Dealin'

*Re*hab is *re*learning – relearning how to live again. From scratching your head to eating a banana; from drinking a glass of water without drowning to eating a salad with a fork; from moving an inch an hour to an inch a minute, then finally the length of a hallway. In essence, Rehab is reclaiming the ordinary functions of daily life.

Rehab, or rehabilitation, is derived from words whose original root meanings combine to convey "to re-inhabit" and "to restore" – to go back to where you were or how you were before an accident or injury. Whether your injury is physical, mental, emotional or spiritual, "rehab" is all about relearning, restoring and returning. True rehab goes further than that, however. True rehab means becoming better than ever; "citius, altius, fortius4 (faster, higher, stronger)" – even if you aren't in the Olympics!

Some days are tougher than others. I will not minimize the struggle and the frustration of rehab, but for the most part, I enjoy the challenge. True to the doctors' predictions, my biceps begin to respond. With increasingly operational arms, and functional shoulders, I get my hands on the wheels of my manual chair, lock my elbows, lean forward in kind of a controlled fall, contract my biceps and using my dysfunctional forearms as levers, I inch my wheelchair forward.

Learning to handle a wheelchair and dealing with my new circumstances, I wheel and deal my way from survival to success. At least, that is my intention.

---

4 Motto of the Olympic Games

Contrary to popular assumption, being quadriplegic doesn't mean you are totally immobile. Quadriplegia simply means that all four limbs – arms and legs – are compromised. Due to accident, injury or illness, they don't function as well as they used to. Some who suffer from quadriplegia are even able to walk; but, typically, their limbs are dysfunctional, awkward, and their gait unsteady.

In my case, because of the fractured vertebrae in my neck, there was damage to the nerves that signal motion to my limbs and signal back to the brain what is going on. I am, therefore, quadriplegic. The purpose of rehab is to discover how much mobility I have left, what I will regain, and adjust for what is lost.

The therapy room is about the size of a basketball court. It is filled with exercise equipment of all sorts. Speakers hang from the ceiling, playing lively music to inspire and energize us, or just keep our minds off the difficulty of mastering mundane tasks.

The perimeter is lined with mats for those of us who are profoundly paralyzed. The mats protect us when we fall while attempting to put on socks and shoes and shirts with our teeth and our numb hands.

It is three o'clock on a particularly frustrating Wednesday afternoon. Shondell and I are sitting on a mat. She is steadying me with her hand on my leg – a hand I cannot feel. Frustrated and angry, I am struggling to put on a t-shirt. I keep getting tangled in soft cotton folds that seem to have the weight of sail canvass.

It is tough enough to have to relearn something a two-year-old can do, but to have your beautiful wife watch you struggle with your weakness – well, the frustration is overwhelming. Why did this happen to me? Why must I be helpless and miserable? Why…

The music stops.

Everyone turns to the door. I shrug off the tangled t-shirt, letting it drop to the mat, as I twist my body to look in that direction as well. There stands Elder Neal A. Maxwell, a General Authority in the Church of Jesus Christ of Latter Day Saints.

I whisper to Shondell, "Look! It's Elder Maxwell."

A visit by someone of Elder Maxwell's status is a great honor.

It's like a Catholic being personally visited by a Cardinal. Why is he here?

He pauses in the doorway for a moment and looks about the room, connecting one by one with each individual. I don't know if you can imagine what it means to someone struggling with life to be really looked at, to be really seen. Many smile back at him, others look away.

Elder Maxwell's eyes rest on me and he walks toward us. "You must be Chad Hymas. And this must be Shondell."

He knows our names. He also knows the names of our children. He knows where I served my church mission, and knows the details of my accident. This man has, in fact, come to see me – personally.

"Your mission president from Bangkok, Thailand, called my office this morning," he says. "When I got word, I came as quickly as I could."

He kneels on the mat beside us. The room grows very quiet. Regardless of anyone's particular religious beliefs, this man is well known and greatly respected in our community. He asks if he can give me a blessing.

Such blessings have special meaning and power. Given and received in faith, they bring comfort and healing to the sick. They also bring guidance to the lost and calm to the distressed. Still feeling angry and discouraged, I look down and tell him I don't feel worthy of a blessing.

He assures me that I am.

He asks Shondell to kneel on the floor in front of me and hold me steady. He places his hands on my head and gives me a wonderful blessing of faith and hope. He also prays for the other patients there. He prays for the doctors, nurses and therapists. He prays for Shondell – that she will accept this bitter cup without resentment.

During our visit, Elder Maxwell reveals something very personal. He has leukemia. He has suffered from it for several years. He admits that in the beginning, he asked God why he had to suffer this affliction. He had been called to travel throughout the world and serve God and didn't understand how he could fulfill his calling if he was sick.

He eventually learned through his own experience and prayerful contemplation that his leukemia and my paralysis and every other affliction, and the challenges and problems they present, are part of what helps us appreciate and become more like the Savior. He believes with all his heart that struggles and challenges lead us to knowledge and growth – if we let them.

Elder Maxwell helps me realize that I must look at my situation differently and gain something positive from it. His advice and his blessing help me change my point of view and move in a new direction.

Misti and Shondell
taking a break

Misti Thimpson, my physical therapist, is beautiful inside and out. She is also tough as a crowbar and strong enough to toss my 6'1", 180-lb. frame around like a rag doll when she needs to.

Misti doesn't just come to work for a paycheck. Her purpose is to serve and to make a difference in the quality of life of her patients. That she does. She helps me understand that I am quadriplegic, but not *a* quadriplegic. Understanding the difference makes a huge difference in my rehabilitation.

Like Shondell, Misti doesn't give up on me or let me give up on myself. She is tough. But she isn't a drill sergeant. Her encouragement cancels discouragement. Her faith in me inspires faith in myself. She is, in fact, the quintessential inspirational leader. *She inspires me to live up to her expectations, not give in to my deprivations.*

Like an eager child wanting to impress my pre-school teacher, I practice over and over again. I want to show her that I can put on a t-shirt or my socks by myself. When it doesn't work, I try again and again – and then again. If it still doesn't work, I feel suddenly tired. Not just tired – soul-weary. A black flood of discouragement pours into me. I am not a child, I am a man. This isn't fun; this is frustrating. This isn't challenging; this is depressing. I want to give up. Just give up.

But in a moment of quiet and supportive reassurance, combined with infinite patience and unwavering faith, Misti infuses me with new determination. She helps me with some little improvement in my approach – or the use of a tool or technique – or a coping mechanism. I take one more small but wonderful step towards independence.

I hate learning to use the manual wheelchair, though. There is nothing about it that is fun. It's drudgery. It's distressing. It's painfully difficult, with painfully slow progress.

Every day Misti nudges me forward. She is firm and gently encouraging in the same moment. She says, "You can do this, Chad. I know it. You may not believe it, but I do. You have the right attitude."

If I manage to move the wheelchair even one more foot further than the day before, she makes a really big deal out of it! You'd think I had won the Boston marathon. She laughs delightedly, she hops up and down – she gets teary-eyed.

"Look, Chad, another foot!" I mock her by looking down to see if I have three feet. She rolls her eyes and smiles. She isn't being condescending. She knows – somehow, she really knows – how hard it is for someone in my condition to make that kind of progress and have a sense of humor about it. It's easier to succeed when Misti is rooting for me. She is right there beside me like a healing angel breathing spirit into my broken body. With all the faith in me that I may not have in myself – she makes magic happen.

Pushing, pushing, pushing that wheeled torture device – five feet this week, seven feet the next week, then ten. Then the length of the hall...

This is my career now, my new profession, my full time job. Five hours a day, Monday through Friday, starting at eight in the morning with a two hour break for lunch. On Saturdays I have just an hour of therapy. Sundays are days of rest.

Enter now, Ron Honey. He is my occupational therapist. Ron has me stacking blocks, playing Checkers, Risk, Monopoly and Monotony (made that one up) and other board games to improve my manual dexterity. We play the same game over and over again – hence, "Monotony."

Chad with Ron Honey

Ron is a powerfully built red-head – with a wee bit of temper, especially when he gets on my case. It seems strange that he is the occupational therapist and the slighter, smaller Misti is the physical therapist. "Ron the Hun" might be a better name. Straightforward and direct, he is just what I need.

Ron teaches me how to eat with a fork, how to type, and how to shave. He shows me how to button a shirt with my teeth and how to pull my pants up with numb fingers and hands. He molds a fiberglass brace that fits over my hand and wrist. He attaches a metal fork or a spoon – and this gizmo works. I practice by putting the spoon into a bowl of rice, then lifting it to my mouth with a mound of rice that steadily diminishes in size until only one grain of rice reaches my disappointed lips. Eventually, I get all the food into my mouth instead of everywhere else. I use this brace for a month or two. I soon discover that, if someone puts a fork or spoon in my hand in a certain way, I don't need the brace.

Though I have no feeling in my fingers, I do have some kind of sensation. It is a sense of pressure or resistance. It helps me know what is going on. As the doctor's predicted, my wrists begin to work. If I lift my hand in the air and, using my now operational wrist, turn it palm upward, the fingers automatically curl and create a grip.

Try it – see what your hands do. Relax your fingers and turn your palm upward. See how your fingers clench? The more relaxed your hand, the firmer your grasp.

If I can maneuver something like a felt tip marker or an eating utensil into my hand and entwine it in my fingers, I can maintain a fairly firm grip on it. This phenomenon allows me to hold a marker to sign books with, or a fork or spoon to eat with. If I can scoop a sandwich up between my forefinger and thumb, I can raise it to my mouth.

I also learn how to type with the aid of a typing tool. It fits over and around the hand, but is open enough for me to push my hand into it. A long straight stick protrudes from the device and allows me to type using the good ol' "hunt and peck" method.

At first, typing the simple phrase, "I love you," takes me a full minute. That's an impressive three words a minute. It isn't because I am slow at hitting the keys. It's because I have to figure out how to lift up my arm – a difficult task in itself – after I lightly touch the correct key. *Lightly* touching the key – is the key.

I can't *feel* what I am doing, so I have to *watch* what I am doing. I don't mean watch the key; I mean, watch the monitor. If I hold the key down too long, I get this: llll lllooovvve yooouuuu. If I happen to be using one of those computers with a voice program for the visually impaired, it sounds like Woody Woodpecker.

At the writing of this book, I type about fifty-four words per minute, depending on the length of the words. I love the sentence "If it is to be, it is up to me," not just because it is philosophically profound, but because that's ten words I can type fast.

I actually type faster than I could before the accident. I can, and do, answer all my own emails. Isn't that great!

Of course, that's because I never learned how to type before the accident.

Ron teaches me to pick up a paper cup with one hand and drink from it; take the paper cover off a straw using my wrists and teeth; and cut my food (ah, finally, steak and potatoes) with a knife.

He teaches me to comb my hair. At first this takes me several minutes. I can now comb my hair in zero minutes – since I started shaving my head! Hey, if Sean Connery and Bruce Willis can do it and maintain their sex appeal, so can I.

I shave by putting shaving cream on my wrist and applying it to my whiskers. Using a special device, I get a grip on the razor and lift it to my face. After an hour of this, I wash the shaving cream off my face, get my electric shaver, and am done in 60 seconds!

I learn to brush my teeth – and my lips and my nose. I talk on the phone by pushing the speakerphone button or yell into my lap where I have dropped my cell phone. Passersby look politely in the other direction.

I write my name illegibly. No change there.

My kids are great motivators. Christian and Kyler love the light-weight, red therapy ball which is twice the size of a basketball. They toss it to me and I try to punch it back toward them with my elbows. I am not very good at it, but they think it is great fun.

It is fun. It is also humbling. I am the dad. I am supposed to teach *them* how to play ball. Instead, *they* are teaching *me*.

I begin to understand an important element of success, taught by Machiavelli. He suggested that we build our teams carefully for they reflect on us and we gain greatness from the skill and reputation of the great ones we surround ourselves with.

I am blessed with an incredible Executive Committee. My amazing children and our CMO (Chief Mommy Officer), Shondell.

I didn't just choose them; they also chose me. I am twice blessed!

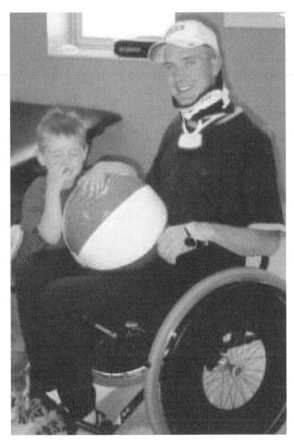

The most difficult thing is the decision to act; the rest is merely tenacity. The fears are paper tigers. You can do anything you decide to do. You can act to change and control your life; and the procedure, the process is its own reward.

~Amelia Earhart

Ten

Tenacity

Winston Churchill insisted that the key to success is to simply never give up. If that is true, I must be a failure. I do give up. I get tired. I get discouraged. And I quit!

I quit a lot.

Sometimes, I quit once or twice a day.

However, I don't stay quit. That's what is important. My family doesn't quit on me, either. They are dedicated to my recovery. Shondell is here with me every day, all day long, six days a week. She takes Sunday off to be with our kids and attend to her church duties.

Mom has taken a ten-week leave of absence from her job to be with me and to take care of the kids when Shondell is with me in rehab. Dad comes by every day during his lunch hour to see how I'm doing. His wife, Terrie, comes with him, unless she is helping out with the kids. They say it takes a village to raise a child. That is true in my case – to raise me a second time.

My brothers visit three or four times a week. They encourage me repeatedly to focus on the little things and let the big things take care of themselves. They remind me how I taught them the same thing on the job. "Little things taken care of take care of the big things." I was their manager. Now I am being managed.

When speaking of his success as a speaker, author and family man, my mentor, Art Berg, said, *"I am not in my current successful circumstances by any one big grand event. It's the little things I've chosen to do every single day, that bring about the greatest results in my life."*

Losing the function of most of my body is not acceptable to me. I want miraculous improvements – now! It doesn't happen that way. To get where I want to go is a struggle. Bit by bit, inch by inch, I do the little things, the possible, the achievable, to one day get the big things *DOne.*

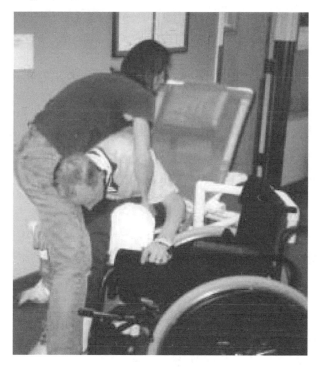

Shondell must lift me without hurting herself. I help as much as I can.

Another thing Misti stresses in rehab is the importance of staying healthy. All the wonderful plans in the world will not move a broken down machine – therefore, I must stay as fit and healthy as possible.

I wear long johns – sometimes two pair – when it is chilly because my body thermostat is out of whack and I am very susceptible to cold. I wear a knit hat in the winter to help avoid getting sick, like I did in 2005. I was on a speaking tour in Saginaw, Michigan, having just delivered the keynote address for the Michigan Health and Safety Conference. I sat too long on the tarmac at the airport, waiting to board a commuter plane. It was January and freezing cold. I was not dressed warmly enough and wasn't wearing a hat. So I got pneumonia.

Bad for you. Deadly for me.

It took a long time to recover.

Some people, when they leave rehab, seem to forget everything they were taught about eating healthy. They go back to their old habits. Not me. I'm careful to not over-eat. I avoid sweets. I take either a vitamin C or a cranberry tablet every day to maintain digestive and bladder health. I eat two good meals a day. I focus on protein. I drink lots of liquids.

Managing bladder and bowel waste elimination is a major issue. It is something I really don't like to talk about; but it is one of those fundamental issues that those with quadriplegia and paraplegia must deal with.

I hate using a leg bag. Though covered by my slacks, it still seems unsanitary and I worry about odor. Shondell rinses it out nightly with bleach, but I still think it smells. Other people have learned to live with it, but it isn't for me, so I learn to cath' myself. I innovate. I cut off the end of a catheter and attach it to a three-foot length of surgical tubing. I can hang the tubing over into a toilet or in a used water bottle and let it drain.

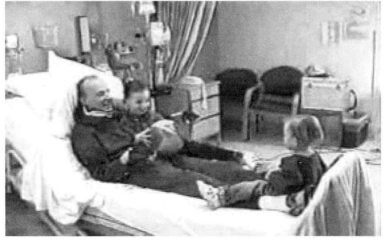

Now, three kids for Shondell

I monitor how much goes in, so I know when it's time to let waste out. My dad is a little squeamish about this. Since I am numb from the upper chest down, cath'ing isn't a problem, but Dad cringes and leaves the room. I drink bottled water and use the empty water bottles for waste. My family has learned which water bottle not to drink from!

Freeing myself from the leg bag may seem like a small thing, but it was a major step for me. Like most major steps in life, it wasn't easy. Learning to measure intake, so I knew when to drain is painstaking and I had lots of accidents. I hated "potty training", but again, as in business or in life, a simple task mastered gives us greater control over the more complex tasks; greater power over one's circumstances and, ultimately, greater freedom.

Like other two-year-olds, potty training gives me a sense of independence. After finally getting rid of the leg bag, I attend a family barbecue – wearing shorts for the first time since my accident. Mom notices right away. "Where's the bag?" she whispers. I just grin. She is as proud of me as I am of myself.

Yes, I am a big boy now, but Mom is still important. One day, I am on my way to a meeting and want to cath' myself beforehand. My zipper is stuck and, even with the nifty innovative bailing wire invention Art Berg helped me design, I can't get a grip on it. I drive to Mom's office and phone her from my van. "Mom, I need your help. My zipper is stuck."

She is there ASAP taking care of me. As much as I appreciate this, I hate having to be taken care of. But, when one is trouble, thank God for moms.

Do you think I am making too big a deal of this bathroom stuff? I'm not. It is a big deal to those who deal with quadriplegia. Confucius said, "A journey of a thousand miles begins with one step." Every step of the journey is important, the first step just as important as the last. Nothing comes without effort. It is four months before I can put on a shirt. It's eight months before I can brush my own teeth, shave, eat by myself, or pick up a telephone.

Chad putting on a shirt

Using the phone

A full year passes before I can undress myself. It takes hours the first time I try. I can now get undressed by myself in twenty-three minutes. It probably takes you three minutes or less, but I'm proud of my twenty-three minutes.

It is fourteen months before I get my driver license back and eighteen months before I travel to my first speaking engagement by myself. Previously, I have always taken a nurse, Shondell, or a brother with me. My first solo trip is to Irvine, California. This is when I realize just how independent I can be and how great it feels to be free again.

Several times a year, Misti calls me and asks me to come and visit the rehab unit. I go as often as I can. I'm grateful for this chance to encourage the patients, especially the new ones. I pay special attention to those who do not have the same family support that I do. It is my way of repaying those who made my new life possible.

Misti and her husband, Matt, have become close friends. We enjoy attending basketball games as couples. It gives her a chance to check up on me now and then. She says I am still her favorite two-year-old.

Today I am my own rehab therapist. I regularly stretch out all the muscles that no longer work. I do this morning and night while on the bed. If I am home, Shondell moves my legs to keep them flexible. I lift weights to strengthen my wrists, biceps and shoulders. From the shoulders up, I'm bulked up!

Pushing my chair is rehab. Getting dressed and undressed is rehab. Brushing my teeth and shaving is rehab. Everything I do is rehab. Rehab for me is perfecting the daily tasks – the mundane, repetitive tasks of life – so that I can keep going, learning and doing new things.

Focus on the essential tasks with your mind's eye on the prize. Make it a habit. You will be amazed at what you can do and what you ultimately get *DOne*.

A man is but the product of his thoughts…
what he thinks, he becomes.

~Mohandas Ghandi

Eleven

Blame Game

To regret the experience is to regret the lesson – because the lesson is inextricably contained in the experience. Too often when changes occur and our circumstances are not as we planned, we tend to focus on what we lost, what we've missed, what's gone wrong, who is to blame, and "why me." We are not accepting the reality of our changed circumstance *or the opportunity those changed circumstances present*. We ignore the gift of change and delay our progress.

A certain amount of "Dang, I just shouldn't have done that," is natural; and accepting the fact that you did it – or failed to do it – is healthy. *But spending too much time in regret denies us the opportunity of getting the most out of our experience – devastating though the experience may seem.* By accepting the reality of my experience and the opportunity to gain what I can from both the experience *and the result*, I gain the blessing of focusing on new opportunity and getting on with my life.

In his book, "The Impossible Just Takes a Little Longer," Art Berg wrote, "Life changes. It is the nature of life to do so. For those in this life who choose not to change, life will change for you. And it is always more painful that way." Life has changed for my family and me. However uncomfortable that change may be, it is up to me to decide how to respond.

I initially reacted to my accident – and especially to the resulting difficult circumstances – first with blame, then with regret.

What should my response be now? How about asking questions? Then ask better questions. Doesn't asking better questions bring better answers? I need to stop asking why this happened to me. It happened, because I was in a hurry. I failed to put hydraulic fluid into the reservoir. The hydraulics failed and a one-ton bale of hay landed on me and broke my neck. I need to ask the larger question. Did this happen for a purpose – or can I create a purpose for what has happened?

"That was then; this is now" isn't just some trite statement tossed flippantly about to avoid dealing with something. It is an important phrase. What has happened has happened. Why it happened is good for our learning and development, but not worth two cents if we just use it to beat ourselves up. Instead of "why," ask "how" or "what." *How* did it happen? *What* will happen now? *How* do I deal with it? *How* will I turn the circumstances of the accident, even my loss of mobility, to an advantage? *What* will I do to be more productive and successful?

You've heard it said that, "necessity is the mother of invention." It is also true that deprivation is the father of innovation. It was obvious that in order to survive and succeed, I needed to innovate. What can I do differently? What can I do today to get done what I need to get done tomorrow, when I can't do it the way I did it yesterday?

I do not mean, what can I do differently just to avoid future mistakes. I mean, what can I do to take advantage of new circumstances brought on by my mistakes – or the mistakes of others? Isn't it true that when circumstances prevent us from doing something the way we have always done it, we are forced to innovate? Isn't it also true that the new way of doing things is often better?

So, how can I *respond* to my paralysis and pain constructively, rather than *react* destructively? How can I use my experience of dealing with paralysis to enhance my ability to deal with other life challenges? Maybe I can use my experience to enhance life itself – the meaning of life – by helping others deal with *their* challenges?

Being quadriplegic, I periodically suffer involuntary muscle spasms in my legs. These spasms are painful, though not painful to my legs – because I can't feel them – but generally painful. When a spasm occurs, it causes the muscle in my chest to contract and I can't take a full breath. The other three chest muscles that are "paralyzed" then kick in and involuntarily contract, or do whatever they feel like doing, and it feels like I am suffocating. It hurts everywhere. When it first happened, I thought I was going to die.

These muscle spasms are significant. If I'm not careful when quadriceps or other large muscle groups fire involuntarily, the spasm can dump me out of my wheel chair. The typical reaction of the medical community to these spasms suffered by paralytics is to deal with the problem by *getting rid* of the problem. Most paraplegics and quadriplegics, therefore, take prescription medication to get rid of the spasms. That seems like a smart thing to do.

However, is it possible that the muscle spasms, as painfully uncomfortable as they are, could be an asset? What if we could get "rid of a problem" such as this – not by stopping the physical reaction – but by turning the problem to our advantage? We could thereby transform a problem into a possibility – a liability into an asset.

Sure enough, I discovered a practical and important use for those irritating muscle spasms. When instigated on purpose, at the right time and in the right way, those uncomfortable spasms help me dress myself.

With my numb thumbs and my teeth, I create an opening in a sock wide enough for my foot to enter. I place the opening of the sock around my toes, and then trigger a spasm by hitting my knee. My foot starts bouncing up and down and works its way into the sock. It takes six or seven minutes just to get one sock on – but I can dress myself.

Instead of being an inconvenience, those spasms are an extremely important asset that has increased my independence significantly. Being able to dress myself might sound like a silly little thing to talk about in an inspirational book – but it is a huge victory for me. Why? Because I can do for myself what used to take a team to do for me.

It also provided a fun way to torment my mother. A few months after my accident I got my legs quivering and bouncing and hollered, "Mom, come here quick! Look! I can move my legs!"

She nearly fainted.

To put on my pants, I stick my thumbs inside the belt loops and, with my partially functioning arms, lift up and shove my legs, one at a time, inside the leg openings. I then jump-start the spasm and by rocking my body back and forth with my thumbs maintaining the upward pull, my pants bounce on.

I've had to change the types of shoes I wear. (I sure do miss my running shoes and cowboy boots.) Today I wear slip-on shoes. They are a size too large so that, with the help of a spasm, my feet bounce in. This process takes only a minute per shoe.

I used to use the spasm in my arm to autograph my books and posters. That was easy because an autograph could be just a squiggle – the more illegible, the more famous you must be!

Now, I can actually write a fairly legible sentiment to the reader and sign my name "Chad." Sure glad my Mom didn't name me "Garfunkle" or "Gustafsen." I would only be able to autograph three books an hour.

I dress myself. I brush my teeth. I feed myself. I drive a car.

I guess I am not disabled.

Neither is Ari Seirlis.

Who is Ari Seirlis?

He is the national director of the Quadriplegic Association of South Africa. He was injured in a diving accident. He now devotes much of his time to promoting better accessibility for those in wheelchairs. Ari Seirlis refuses to refer to himself as "disabled."

"I'm quadriplegic," he says, "but that doesn't mean I am disabled. *You* decide whether you are disabled. *You* decide whether you are confined to a wheelchair or whether it is a tool of mobility. You will never find the phrase 'I am confined to a wheelchair' coming out of my mouth."

People with such constructive thinking help us focus on our abilities, not our disabilities or limitations. I am quadriplegic, but I am not *a* quadriplegic. Ari Seirlis is right.

I am Chad.

Life is not determined by
what happens to me,
but by how I respond to what happens.
It is not about what life brings to me;
but what I bring to life.

~ *Anonymous*

Twelve

Freedom Is Not Independence

Being home isn't as grand as I imagined it would be while I was in rehab. I soon learn how confined my existence is. I can't do what I used to. I can't go feed the elk. I can't run my ranch or my landscaping business. I have no idea how to make a living to support my family.

For the first time in my life, I am bored. Excruciatingly, painfully bored. I lie on my bed for days wondering what to do with the rest of my life – no, the rest of my day – or maybe just the next minute.

I watch television for hours. Judge Judy becomes my best friend.

One sunny afternoon, I sit moping in my wheelchair. Court is in recess until tomorrow. Judge Judy has abandoned me. Shondell loaded me in my chair earlier, and now I sit by the living room window, watching her play basketball with our two boys.

My wife is teaching my son how to jump off the left foot and shoot with the right hand. That was supposed to be my job. They are laughing, shouting, and having a great time – without me.

Shondell misses a basket. Christian gets the rebound.

That is something I should be doing. I'm supposed to be the coach. I'm the one who should be teaching my sons how to play ball. I have two choices. I can continue to sit in the sun where it is comfortable and safe – and boring – or I can choose to change.

I choose to change.

I slowly turn my chair towards the door. As my chair turns around, so does my life. I lean into the task, pushing myself slowly across the carpeted living room. Moving a wheelchair over carpet is far from easy, especially when your arms and hands don't work so well. It takes me ten long minutes to move those few feet to the front door. The team is in the fourth quarter by the time I manage to shove the latch down.

I awkwardly push open the door, and wheel myself out onto the porch. Shondell and my two boys stop and look at me.

"Can I play?" I ask, hesitantly.

Chad and family playing Nerf basketball

Christian, my constant hero, jumps up and down and yells, "Yay, Dad!"

Shondell just smiles.

I wheel carefully down the ramp and onto the cement court. Christian drops a blue Nerf ball onto my lap and waits while I get a grip on it with my wrists.

Shondell drags over Kyler's three-foot-high Nerf basket to where I sit and I make a basket.

One small basket for Dad; one giant leap for Chad.

Then Christian makes a basket. Then Shondell makes a basket.

Then one-year-old Kyler, who has also been watching from the sidelines, gets to make a basket.

I learn something new. This ex-basketball team captain learns something about the real game of life, and the power of a team who understands that everyone deserves to score.

Playing a game where everyone can win is the best game of all.

As we play in the wonderful heat of that amazing mid-summer day, I realize that my life is not determined by what happens to me, but by how I respond to what happens. It is not about what life brings to me, but rather what I bring to life. This thought is pivotal.

Thoughts are powerful. A change in our thinking changes our lives. Whether mystical or natural, one new thought can cause a chain reaction, creating new events and new outcomes. New thinking creates new assumptions. New assumptions create different feelings and attitudes. New attitudes create a new approach to old challenges. A new approach creates new circumstances.

Change is not always easy, though. Even a change for the better can cause us to feel uncomfortable and unbalanced. Replacing a habit or a belief requires diligent effort. Like anyone going through a traumatic ordeal, I have to make significant changes in order to survive and move forward. Most importantly, I have to change the way I think.

I have always prided myself on my independence. I was the guy my family and friends could always call on when they needed something. I am now the one who needs help. Actually, I have always needed help. I just didn't realize it.

We live in a ranching community. Ranchers and farmers depend on each other for their livelihood – rounding up animals that have slipped through holes in fences, branding cattle, tilling fields, and bringing in the harvest. There are horses and elk to feed, alfalfa hay to plant, cultivate and harvest. There are newborn elk that must be tagged.

Freedom is not independence – it never was. Employees, neighbors, family and friends are a part of my team and essential to my success. I am, and always have been, dependent on them. My success never was and never will be "my" success; it always was and always will be "our" success. I cannot succeed on my own – that is a *good* realization. I never could – that is a *great* realization.

Since my accident, I need help more than ever – and I don't have to ask. Whether it is spring planting or fall harvest, neighboring ranchers and their families arrive early and stay until the job is done. It is still very difficult for me to be more of an observer and less a participant; however, I have gotten better at graciously and humbly accepting the help of others.

Because of my innate desire to be as independent as possible, I prefer to drive wherever I go. That requires the help of others. Depending on others in order to be independent? That sounds like a contradiction, doesn't it? I can drive just fine, but how do I get in or out of my vehicle? Shondell can help get me into the driver's seat, but what happens at the other end of the trail? Once I reach my destination, I have to find someone to help me transfer to my wheelchair.

When I am on a speaking engagement, it is even more complicated. I need help getting out my laptop and setting up equipment. I need assistance with nearly everything necessary for me to do my job. I get help from complete strangers. Often they are people who are not involved with the event and who have no idea who I am.

Asking for help is made easier because people are willing to help. They even seem to appreciate the opportunity. Drivers of limos, SUVs, taxis, and shuttles, handle my bags, lift me out of vehicles, position me carefully in my wheelchair and make sure I get where I need to go. Hotel staff members make certain that I have everything I need in my room. They transfer me to the bed – I can't transfer myself if the bed is more than four inches above the wheel height of the chair. They make sure that my computer is plugged in and my communications are handy and operational. They check in on me periodically to make sure I am okay.

Not only do professionals go out of their way to accommodate me, so do perfect strangers. My freedom depends on kindness – the kindness of strangers. I have traveled all over the world – often by myself – and don't worry about getting stuck anywhere. Whether it's a movie theater, restaurant, sports stadium; whether it is in New York, New Hampshire, Africa or Alaska, Houston Texas or Butte Montana; there is always someone ready to help.

Well, almost always.

A couple years after my accident, my family and I go on a family adventure at a popular amusement park. The kids ride every possible ride, as many times as they can. They get along well, except for a couple of sibling meltdowns due to over stimulation and probably too much cotton candy, chocolate covered bananas, and candy apples.

Then I have a meltdown of my own – and it isn't due to sugar overload. We have been on several rides. Staff has transferred me readily and kindly every time from my chair to the ride and back again. Then suddenly, at the end of a ride, the park staff won't transfer me. They have transferred me to the ride, but when the ride is over, they will not transfer me back to my wheelchair. It appears that someone in management has become concerned about potential liability, if they were to drop me and injure me.

My kids get off. My wife gets off. I just sit there in stunned silence. It is too much of a lift for my wife and two small boys. I am overwhelmed with disbelief and frustration, feeling for the first time in a long time helpless and hopeless.

I wonder if I will end up like that poor fellow who allegedly got stuck on the Boston commuter train. They let him on, but they wouldn't let him off because he didn't have another nickel to pay the exit fare.

"Did he ever return?
No he never returned
And his fate is still unlearn'd
He may ride forever 'neath the streets of Boston
He's the man who never returned." 5

---

5 "M.T.A.," often called"The MTA Song," is a 1949 song by Jacqueline Steiner and Bess Lomax Hawes. Known informally as "Charlie on the MTA," the song's lyrics tell of a

Just like Charlie, I might ride forever – on this stupid kiddy ride, round and round until my brain turns to mush. I am angry. Furious. Seething! No one will help. It seems indeed such a small, small world – run by people with small, small minds.

Then, without being asked, three perfect strangers step forward and transfer my 170-pound frame to my chair. "Perfect strangers" is right. Perfectly wonderful, perfectly beautiful, perfectly kind and considerate strangers, giving me perfect love and support.

It's hard enough to feel like you fit in when you are paralyzed. The one thing you don't want to do is to draw any unnecessary attention to yourself – especially to your disabilities. This incident does just that, and three strangers save me from an embarrassing situation.

Have you ever asked yourself what it is someone with a disability might need or want? Next time you see us struggle with some kind of task that wouldn't be difficult for an "able-bodied" person, ask if you can be of service. Just ask. If you see someone having a hard time with a door or a stairway, take a moment to see if you can help – just like you would with someone struggling with an armload of groceries.

Put yourself in our position and do the same thing you would want someone to do for you. Just ask. Help us in the way we ask you to, then move on and don't make a big deal out of it. Say "Hello" as you would to anyone else, as we roll by the water cooler at work. Include us in your chats and invite us to your after-work get-togethers. Do it because you want to. It truly is the right thing to do. You may find that we will be good friends in return – especially if one day a bale of hay falls on *your* head!

It is a major breakthrough for me to learn to accept – and actually depend on – the kindness and generosity of others. It is a big step for me, and necessary for my development. How can we learn to be kind, generous, helpful, or supportive, if we aren't allowed to do that for

---

man named Charlie trapped on Boston's subway system. A version of the song became a 1959 hit when recorded and released by the Kingston Trio, an American folk group.

others? And how can others learn those wonderful traits, if we don't allow them to do it for us – and show our appreciation when they do.

It is right to give,
This we all believe;
But it takes a truly generous heart,
To learn graciously to receive.

I may not ever make it to heaven,
but at least I can say I raised an angel.

~ Joe Barton (Shondell's father)

Thirteen

Angel

Shondell

I married an angel.

On our wedding day, my father says to me, "Chad, you don't deserve this girl."

"I know, Dad, but neither does anyone else, so it might as well be me."

Whether he is serious or kidding, he is right. I don't deserve her. Fact is, I never thought I was good enough for her, even when we were dating. I would never have asked her out. Like I said before, how could a "Chad" ever deserve a "Shondell"?

When she asks me out, I look her up in the yearbook to make certain she really is that beautiful dark-haired girl who teased me in the gym earlier today. Looking over my shoulder at Shondell's yearbook photo, Brian says, "Wow! You better go, Chad. You'll never again get a date with anyone as pretty as she is."

It just so happens, the day she wants to go out with me is my birthday. I am supposed to go to dinner with my family, but I don't want to risk this once-in-a-lifetime opportunity to go out with a girl like Shondell. I change my dinner plans. My family is happy to oblige.

Shondell has been a blessing in my life ever since – in fact she *is* my life. She is an incredible sweetheart, partner and wife. She is an amazing mother. She loves her boys, including me, and our precious little girl, Gracee. No matter what her outside activities or obligations, we always come first.

Nevertheless, Shondell has her own life – and what a life it is. A family friend, Alydia Barton, helps Shondell get started running marathons. She gives Shondell tips on how to train and run. Shondell trains hard for her first half marathon – 13.1 miles. This is August. It is hot. She runs well. At the end of the race, she is delighted to find that she could have kept on running.

Shondell and her team

She immediately seeks out another race – one scheduled for October in San Francisco. It is The Nike 29.2 – that benefits the Leukemia and Lymphoma Society. She talks her sister, Sherrie, into running with her. Sherrie runs the half marathon and Shondell runs the full. They raise several thousand dollars.

The next full marathon is in St. George in October of 2005. Many of Shondell's family members live in that area, so she has great personal support. They hold up posters, encourage her every grueling mile, and cheer her on to the finish. Shondell always goes the extra mile for her family – and now they are here for her.

This particular marathon has special meaning for my wife. Shondell has a friend whose baby daughter had a stroke two weeks before she was delivered. Little Hadley is born with many medical problems. This marathon helps Shondell raise enough money to help this family with medical expenses.

Shondell is heavily involved with "Bridge of Love," a foundation whose mission is to bring hope and relief to the abandon children in Romania. Each October, they sponsor a special community fundraiser to provide decent food, clothing, and shelter for Romanian orphans. These once destitute and abandoned children now laugh, learn, play, and dream of a future full of possibility.

Bridge of Love

Bridge of Love fundraising events are often family affairs. Little ones and adults, alike, run and/or walk the one-mile to 5k course. Times are recorded and prizes awarded for each age-bracket. These are beautiful events, with local and celebrity speakers who address the crowd in a fun and entertaining way, raising awareness and enthusiasm. These events are well publicized and well attended. It is an uplifting, dynamic, community-binding event.

Shondell is not a reflection of these events; rather, these events are a reflection of her. They magnify the heart of my Angel.

Very early one morning, a young man shows up on our doorstep and asks to see me. This seems odd, because our ranch is in the middle of nowhere. This young man heard me speak and wants to meet me personally. He pushes his way into our home when Shondell opens the door. Shondell manages to persuade him to leave. He does so without incident, but it's unsettling to realize how vulnerable we are.

Shondell decides to learn the art of self-defense. She begins with a class in Kamagong, a martial art developed in the Philippines. At first, her plan is simply to gain enough skill to protect herself and her family adequately. She finds, however, that she very much enjoys the exercise and discipline involved. She decides to further her Kamagong training. Shondell is the only female in the class. She ultimately earns the coveted black belt and is inducted into the Philippine Martial Arts Hall of Fame.

Shondell receives her Black Belt

I am now *officially* afraid of her.

Shondell is elected President of the PTA. She is re-elected the next year. That, combined with her duties as a volunteer teacher's aide, has her at the elementary school two or three times a week. Once school is out for the day, her real job begins – taxi driver. She transports our children to scouts, piano lessons, gymnastics, church functions, basketball and soccer practices and games. She also assists the little league basketball coach (me) and takes over my duties when I am away on a speaking assignment.

She recently planned a well-deserved weekend with her mother and sisters in Salt Lake City. She leaves me in charge.

"Chad, can you handle things for me for a day?"

"Sure, honey. Piece of cake."

She is only gone twenty-four hours. Even though she has taken care of a number of things before my "shift," so the activities are limited to about thirty percent of her normal routine, I barely make it through alive. No way can I keep up with her – in anything!

Shondell is soft, sweet and gentle; yet tough as nails and never ceases to work for the good of everyone around her. Her father said it best, "I may not make it to Heaven, but at least I can say I raised an angel!"

My career as a professional speaker takes me all around the world. I'm on stage every single week and love telling others what my accident brought to me and to those I serve. People come up to me and say things like, "Chad, you handle your situation remarkably well."

Those comments are appreciated, but what they don't know is that I could handle none of it without Shondell. Her life is greatly impacted by my accident, yet her personal fortitude, patience and great love touch the lives of all who know her.

Still, I hate seeing Shondell having to do all the things I am supposed to do. I don't like her having to drive all the time, get out in the rain to put fuel in the car, mow the lawn, and do the chores. Those should be my jobs. I especially don't like her having to help me use the bathroom, get dressed, and eat. This wasn't part of the marriage contract. It wasn't part of the deal.

It is particularly hard for me in the beginning.

Shortly after I arrive home from rehab, Shondell is helping me transfer to my wheelchair. She loses her grip and drops me. Apologizing softly, she reaches down to help me back up and into my chair. I see a bead of sweat trickle down her cheek. I've had enough. I begin to cry. "Leave me alone," I demand through my tears. "Go away. Leave me on the floor. I don't want your help anymore. I'm done."

I am in torment. Emotional agony. Can you imagine my frustration and humiliation? Why did this happen to me? Why can't I take care of my family? Why can't I take care of myself? Why?

"Why" ceases to be a question and becomes a statement of despair, an assumption, a declaration that it shouldn't have happened It should have remained a question – an honest question of why it happened and what I should to do about it. Not the obvious "why" that I failed to put hydraulic fluid in the tractor, but the larger question, the genuinely seeking "why," that might lead me to the larger answer.

If I keep my question a question, instead of a demand, and stop ranting long enough to listen for an answer, I may learn something. But I don't. I become harsh and mean with Shondell. I am embarrassed to admit it. I say things I don't want to recount, things I don't want to remember. Shondell walks out of the room, leaving me alone with my despair and frustration. In a few moments, I exhaust myself. I run out of words and lie on the floor in a crumpled, impotent, tearful heap.

I hear the phone ring in the other room. It is Shondell's mother, Charlene. Shondell answers the phone. I assume she tells her mom what has happened. Charlene apparently asks to speak to me, because Shondell walks back into the bedroom and silently hands me the phone.

I spend the next hour and a half talking to my mother-in-law. No, I spend the next hour and a half *venting*, pouring out my anger and frustration, my feelings of impotence, my sense of uselessness. My mother-in-law and I have been very close from the day Shondell and I first started dating – so I let it all out, recounting everything that has just happened. From my undignified position sprawled on the floor, looking and feeling like a puppet with the strings cut, my pent up frustration comes out of me like poison from a lanced boil.

"This is too hard. It isn't fair. This is humiliating. Why me? Why us? Why Shondell? I hate doing this to her. I am not supposed to be fed and cared for like a baby. I am supposed to be the man in the family. I am supposed to take care of her. I'm not going to do this anymore. I'm not! I am done!"

Charlene lets me rant until I am emotionally and physically drained. When it seems the flood has abated, she quietly asks. "Chad, are you through, yet?"

"Yes," I meekly reply.

"Chad, this is the most selfish I've ever seen you. When you say it wasn't part of the deal, you are wrong. Apparently, you've forgotten the promises you made the day you were married." She pauses. "Do you want to know the greatest gift you could give my daughter?"

"What's that?"

"You can give her your most gracious acceptance."

This hits me like a locomotive. I realize I had just done the very thing the doctor warned me about two months earlier. He told me that she wouldn't likely leave me; but if I wasn't careful, I would push *her* away. I just did it. I pushed Shondell away – and I pushed hard.

Fortunately, my wife is tough. Even more fortunately, she is forgiving.

Gracious acceptance, gracious acceptance – the words keep echoing in my head. Overcoming pride is not easy, but I'm learning. I thank my wife every day for all she does and for who she is. I mean it from my heart. I am grateful beyond words for her love, patience, support and belief in me.

Shondell is my soulmate, my best friend. In the movie *Jerry Maguire,* Tom Cruise told Renee Zellweger. "You complete me."

My Shondell does more than that – she *enhances* me. To her, I am not broken or incomplete. To her, I am a "real man," her man, still and always. Her inspiration and support is the foundation of the success I enjoy today.

I married an angel.

Our doubts are traitors
and make us lose the good we oft might win,
by fearing to attempt.

~ William Shakespeare

Fourteen

Dating Game

Would you think less of me if I told you I went on a date – but not with my wife? What if I told you my wife knew all about it – and that she approved? What if I told you she helped set it up?

Actually, she helps set *me* up!

It is an amazing autumn day. Intense sunlight filters through the blazing red, orange and gold of the aspens and maples adorning the canyons walls in the beautiful Oquirrh and Wasatch mountains. I am ready to roll out and greet the new day. But, wait, what is this?

My electric wheelchair is missing.

I frequently use an electric wheelchair. I have learned to use a manual, because it is better for me physically. Still, I love my black and silver souped-up ride, especially to traverse more difficult terrain. It's like four-wheeling around the ranch.

This sweet machine boasts not one but two supercharged motors – twin engines, man – four-on-the-floor, (okay it's got electric motors and a toggle switch) genuine black leather bucket seats (okay, one seat). It blasts along at thirty-five miles-per-hour. It represents independence and freedom…

…and it's gone!

If this is someone's idea of a joke, I'm not laughing.

I haven't long to ponder the situation. Dad and my two brothers converge on my bedroom. They dress me in jeans and an old sweater. They pick me up like a sack of potatoes and carry me out to the truck.

Aha! There's my chair. The mystery is solved. However, it's no longer a sleek black and silver ride. My family has sand-blasted the thing and painted it the muted brown, green and crème of fall camouflage.

Do they think you can do whatever you want with a rented wheelchair?

I have no time to protest. They load me and my once beautiful power chair into our four-wheel-drive Dodge diesel truck and off we go to Indian Canyon – camouflaged gear (and chair), hunting rifles ammo and all. What on earth are they thinking? Taking me hunting? What part of "paralyzed" do they not understand?

As it turns out, they understand a lot more than I give them credit for.

It has long been a dream of mine to raise elk with my dad. Elk preserves were legalized in Utah in 1999. We went to the legislature the year before to explain the value of the project. When the law was passed that allowed us to do so, Shondell and I didn't wait to act. There were only twenty-seven ranches that raised elk in the state at the time, all governed by strict laws. The property had to meet certain standards and be approved by an oversight board.

It takes us a year to find the right property. We need to be outside the city limits so we look west and south of Salt Lake in Heber, Park City, Coalville, Payson, Morgan, Springville, and Hennifer. A friend tells us of a place in Rush Valley, southwest of Salt Lake City. We drive out and look it over. It is a good piece of land, two hundred acres with water, and the price is right. In the spring of 1999, we sign the papers. We build our dream house and, in August, 1999, we move into our new home. In addition to my landscaping business, we now have an elk ranch and our own family home. Life really is great.

That winter we bring in our first forty head of elk over from Colorado. We will keep them on the ranch until they mature and are ready for transfer to a hunting preserve. That is what we need to find next. A hunting preserve. Dad and I lease a place near Price, Utah, two hours southeast of Salt Lake City. It's fifty-six hundred fenced acres – nine square miles – the largest preserve in the western United States.

We begin building an eight-foot fence around the property, using high tensile steel wire. Elk can jump over anything lower. We complete six miles. There are many miles to go.

Then I am injured.

Dad quits his insurance business and works full time developing the property and promoting the business.

Hunters come from all over the country for a four-day hunt. They fly into Salt Lake International Airport and are driven two hours to our hunting preserve. They stay in heated, walled tents. A chef cooks their meals. The hunting preserve is in the heart of Utah's high country. This wild and rugged land has several large open areas and wooded draws. Professional guides use all terrain vehicles to bring the hunters close to where the game is. The bulls in this hunting area generally range from 300 to 380 on the Boone and Crockett scoring system.

The hunting season goes from early September through the end of November. During the months of January through April, Dad travels from California to Massachusetts, to find clients.

When Dad proposed continuing this project, I didn't say much. I was still in intensive care, if you recall, and *couldn't* say much. I appreciated his enthusiasm, but I didn't think I could be a part of that dream any longer.

My dad and my brothers think differently.

While being bundled into camouflage gear and stuffed into a truck with my color-coordinated wheelchair, I get it! I am going hunting again. I'm so excited! Don't know how I will hold a rifle or pull the trigger, but I am sure Dad will come up with something. Sure enough, he does come up with something.

We soon arrive at our wooded destination. They drag me out of the cab and buckle me into the chair. Then they sprinkle elk cow urine on my head! See the kind of respect I get? Now I know why I was invited to go hunting. What do you think my job is? Elk bait? Not exactly. Not elk *bait* – elk *mate!* There's a big difference.

You don't bait elk. Elk aren't fish. They don't respond to bait. They come in for one reason. What do you think that is? That's right.

They aren't stupid; they are *romantic*!

They put me behind a brush line stinking to high heaven with elk "perfume." I am surprised they don't adorn me with lipstick and a dress.

My dad and brothers then move off a short distance and climb into what they call "a tree stand." Soon they are comfortably perched fifteen feet in the air, in chair-like contraptions secured to the main trunk of something that more closely resembles a telephone pole than a tree. They get out their elk whistles and start to call, hoping to attract a bull elk into sniffing range.

Now, when elk call each other for a date, they don't use mobile phones, they whistle. Kind of like sailors, only both the bull and the cow whistle to each other. They call it elk whistling – because that's what it is. The bull's call is also referred to as "bugling."

Here I sit, nervously awaiting my "date," while my dad and brothers gleefully blow on their elk whistles, trying to attract the biggest, baddest dude in the forest. I am only three-feet-two-inches tall in lumpy camouflage and on wheels. I look a lot like ET but, with my Chanel #5 Elk perfume, I am apparently quite attractive to an elk on a Saturday night.

An uncomfortable feeling washes over me. No, I'm not shy. I'm on the ground. My kinfolk are sitting fifteen feet up, out of danger. Are you getting the picture, dear reader? It's not nice to fool Mother Nature. It is also not very smart to fool a bull elk. They are deadly when they are angry. There is nothing more magnificent than a sleek, healthy, twelve-hundred-pound bull elk in his natural habitat. There's also nothing more frightening than that same big bad bull coming at you with love-light in his eyes. Remember, I am in a wheelchair and don't move very fast. It wouldn't take much for an amorous or angry elk to catch me.

My dad starts bugling. He's good at the "Dating Game." He calls. Then waits. Playing hard to get, I suppose. Then my brother chimes in. He sounds like an old steamboat with a leaky valve. He gives up. My dad keeps making periodic calls.

Finally, a response. It's a little louder, a little longer, a little deeper. It's a bull elk, a nice big one. How do we know? His bugle is deep pitched and drawn out.

His antlers break timberline. Beautiful. An elk's set of horns is called a rack – and this guy has quite a rack. Six points on the left and seven on the right.

These racks are beautiful. You can see them mounted over a huge rock fireplace in a mountain resort reception room. They are quite valuable. A sixteen-point rack with a forty-eight inch spread can bring ten- or twelve-thousand dollars on the open market.

By the way, for you animal lovers out there, you don't have to kill the elk to get the rack. Just wait until spring and find a set that has fallen off. Elk typically shed their antlers in February or March. Of course, finding a complete pair is the trick. Both sides of the pair usually don't fall off at the same time, so they won't be sitting next to each other just waiting to be collected.

Anyway, back to the bull. He's magnificent. He's also formidable. My loyal protective family stays in the tree.

The bull is getting close. Too close. My dad shakes a tree limb. He thinks he's helping. He isn't. I am in mortal danger of becoming a bride.

Then the bull catches human scent – and is gone.

Why does Dad take me hunting and leave me on the ground as date bait? What is his purpose? To bag a prize bull?

Nope. It is to show me, without preaching, that life is not over. To re-inspire me. To re-instill me with passion. Passion for hunting? No. Passion for life. To let me know that I still am, or can be, involved in "normal" activities. I can do things with my family and friends just like before, as long as I am willing to do those things differently – like sitting around in camouflage colors and elk perfume.

A counselor would call this re-socialization. Getting back in touch and interacting with friends, family and associates. Keeping old friendships and making new ones, not as a quadriplegic, but as a person.

I don't know how deeply my father and brothers think through this; after all, they're just good ol' country boys. But what they do is actually amazing. Who in their right mind takes an eighty-percent-paralyzed person into the outback on a hunting trip? Who spray paints a brand new rented electric wheelchair camouflage colors? Who leaves said quadriplegic and said chair right in front of an amorous and soon-to-be-disappointed bull elk?

People who care, that's who.

These people see beyond the disability. They consider the disability to be just a circumstance or situation, difficult, but not defining or limiting. I guess you could call what my folks did that day "redneck rehab." Don't get me wrong; my dad and my brothers are far from being rednecks. Jeff Foxworthy says that rednecks are folks who, when they get stopped by a state trooper and asked if they have any I.D., say, "any idee 'bout whut?"

My dad and brothers might not be rednecks, but they are country boys. Maybe it's their down to earth way of dealing with life that causes them to think beyond the norm. Their idea of rehab certainly stretches far beyond the ordinary. I don't know that you would find a recommendation in any Americans with Disabilities Act compliance manual, to turn a quadriplegic into elk bait – or elk date – but it sure works. Once again, I feel like part of the family – part of the team – even though I am now dead last in the pecking order.

What goes up must come down [fast!]

~ Sir Isaac Newton

Fifteen

Rollercoaster

My dad insists that if I want to be a professional speaker, I have to do something more than just survive an accident. I must have a strong message. I must speak from experiences that my audiences will relate to – especially pragmatic corporate audiences and their meeting planners.

"It is a matter of credibility," he tells me. "You have to share experiences and ideas beyond simply being a quadriplegic. In order for a company to want you as a speaker, you must do something that no one else has done."

I decide to do a wheelchair marathon. My mentor, Art Berg did it. I can, too. He set the standard – a world record. He pushed his chair nearly four hundred miles, a daunting distance for anyone in a wheelchair, conceptually impossible for a quadriplegic. But he did it. He set a record. I can, too. I will stand on his shoulders and extend my reach. In so doing, I extend his reach, because he set the stage. That could give me some credibility. Dad agrees.

My mentor makes the impossible possible. Not by showing me exactly how to do it, but by demonstrating that it can be done. Even after his death, Art Berg is my mentor. He inspires me to do what he would be proud of me for doing.

You don't endure a marathon successfully without extensive training. So, for eighteen months, I train for a marathon; not just any marathon, but a world record wheelchair marathon. I am going to do five hundred miles in a wheelchair – five hundred and thirteen to be exact – through desert country. In order for me to accomplish this, it is wise for me to train in the desert. It is as much conditioning as training. I need to get used to the climate. So, off to the desert I go. I head for Las Vegas with Shondell and my brother, Brian in tow.

It is a hot summer day. We are wandering down the Vegas strip. Brian, who has never quite grown up, notices this unique hotel/casino, "New York New York." It is designed to look like the New York City skyline – complete with the Empire State Building and the Statue of Liberty. What really catches our attention is a roller coaster that winds around and through the building.

Brian has to investigate. Feelings of dreadful anticipation creep up from my primal subconscious and I would rather push on, but he thinks otherwise. Shondell is supportive – of Brian! I am outvoted two to one.

The rollercoaster is called the "Manhattan Express." I will soon discover that "express" means more than speed. The rollercoaster starts somewhere inside the bowels of the hotel. It exits the building near the bottom and climbs two hundred and three feet into the air before beginning a precipitous one-hundred-forty-four-foot drop, reaching speeds up to sixty-seven miles per hour.

This ride of insanity goes all the way to the top of the building and then begins its descent at a ninety-degree angle hitting the bottom in a swooping dip. It then goes up – fast – into this double loopety-loop. Your world turns upside down – twice – and so does your stomach! Then it goes through a series of twists, turns, bumps, hills, and disappears back into the hotel. I have never seen anything like it. I stare at it in dread.

My brother looks at me and says, "Chad, doesn't that look like fun?"

I respond, "Ummmm… No?"

Brian then looks at Shondell and announces to her that they will get me on this ride.

She agrees. "Sounds like fun."

"Over my dead body," I say. I don't always think before I speak. This body is about as dead as it gets! I am beginning to notice that I don't have a whole lot to say about what happens to me anymore. For example, my wife will wake me in the morning and say, "Sweetheart, what would you like to wear today"? I tell her the same thing every morning, "Jeans and a T-shirt, please." And then she dresses me however she wants. I have discovered that I now wear outfits.

Well, I have no choice about this ride, either. They take me over to the hotel. They pick me up – chair and all – carry me up a little flight of stairs and set me down at this gate where you get on the rollercoaster. They leave me sitting there. They have to find a supervisor to get permission to put me on the ride.

Let's think this through. If you need a supervisor's permission to go on a ride, you probably shouldn't even be in the line. Right?

While they are gone, I notice a sign. It's a sign from Heaven – a warning sign! "Welcome to the New York, New York Hotel. Home of the Manhattan Express, World's Largest Roller Coaster. Peak Height 412 feet…"

Then I read some more troubling stuff.

"…Speeds May Exceed 70 Miles Per Hour."

In smaller print at the bottom of the sign, it offers even greater encouragement:

"If you are pregnant, have asthma, heart, liver or bladder failure; we strongly suggest that you do not participate on this ride."

Now, as one who deals with quadriplegia, I am fairly certain I have every one of those problems, with the probable exception of pregnancy.

At the bottom of the sign there is a blue line, with a red arrow pointing to that line, with a notice that could save my life.

You have to be a certain height.

This is my lucky day. I am a couple inches shorter than that line.

My brother and wife return with a supervisor. Feigning disappointment, I point to the sign, while speaking gently to Shondell, "Hon, I'm sorry. There's no way I can ride. Look at the rules."

My lovely wife reads the notice, thinks for a moment, then happily responds, "Just wait one second." She walks around to the back of my wheelchair and cranks up the height adjustment. This makes me tall enough to die. I am a defeated man. With a resigned sigh, I sign a waiver saying I won't sue the hotel if something happens to me.

Shondell and Brian lift me out of my wheelchair, carry me to the last car on this infernal train and plunk me down. They say it is the best place for me to sit. They say it will be more fun. They say it will be better for everyone – in case I throw up!

Now, there is a confidence-builder!

They strap me down with a seat belt and a shoulder harness so I won't fall out. Unfortunately, they don't think about the lower half of me.

We exit the building and prepare for the steep climb. An intercom crackles to life and states: "Please keep your arms and legs inside at all times. Enjoy the ride."

And then it hits me. My legs don't work. I have no more control over them than I do my life. How am I supposed to keep them inside? So I instruct my brother, who is sitting beside me, "Brian, you have one job: You hold my legs down. I don't want them exiting this ride at seventy miles an hour!

We fall over a vertical cliff and descend with rapidly increasing speed. We slam into the first loop. Remember what my brother's job is? His only job? To hold my legs down, right? Well, he's forgotten me entirely. He has thrust his arms straight up in the air – and is whooping and hollering like a twelve-year-old. It's obvious that my safety is the furthest thing from his mind.

My left knee smacks me on the cheekbone with the punch of a prizefighter; my knee doesn't feel it, but my face sure does. My right ankle gets caught in the space between the seats in front of us. My brother, realizing what he has done – or rather failed to do – quickly leans over to help me, but it is too late.

We have started up the second loop, and once again Brian flings his arms wildly into the air, whooping and hollering in unbridled joy.

The ride ends with a series of hills and twists and turns, and then, stops on a dime. Like a blob of paralyzed Silly Putty, I slip-slide out from underneath that ineffectual shoulder harness. My seat belt now adorns my neck. Those next in line look around, probably wondering where the occupant has gone.

My wife and brother quickly disentangle me and transfer me back to my wheel chair. They are laughing. I am not.

Remember when I said, "Express means more than speed?" Well, it does.

I realize, as the sign warned, that I am one who should never have been allowed on that ride. Not for my sake necessarily, but for the sake of the next thrill seeker taking my seat.

Now it is my turn to have fun. The biggest thrill for me on that entire ride was seeing the face of the woman who was about to take my vacated seat. "Vacated" also has another and very apt physiological meaning: I do indeed have bladder failure!

Don't worry when you are not recognized, but strive
to be worthy of recognition.

~ Abraham Lincoln

Sixteen

Getting into Guinness

Las Vegas, here I come! After months of training, I am ready for a five-hundred-mile marathon. I'll beat my mentor's three-hundred-mile record by two hundred miles. I'll get into Guinness! I'll be hot stuff! It'll be fun!

Sometimes, my enthusiasm exceeds my reason. But, why not? It'll be easy; after all, I'll be sitting down all the way. I'll plan and execute it like a business goal. Keep it simple. Break the big goal into little goals.

I get out my computer and compute. Doesn't take long. Las Vegas is actually five hundred and thirty-one miles away. I will do fifty-three miles a day and arrive at the Mirage Hotel and Casino in Las Vegas from Salt Lake City in ten days. If I *do* every day what needs to be *done*, I'll get the big thing *DOne*. Five hundred thirteen miles. A world record.

I tell my family about my audacious plan. They are excited. Everyone wants to help. Sometimes, the sheer lunacy of an idea inspires people to get involved. My dad's sister, Christine and her husband, Wayne, are retired and agree to drive the support vehicle, their luxurious motor home. Family and friends promise to join us for moral support whenever they can. Shondell will be with me the entire time and so will my mom and dad. Medical professionals volunteer to accompany us.

I will use Art Berg's specially built three-wheeled hand-driven cycle. I bought it from his family after Art passed away. A pilot car will precede the caravan and we'll be followed by a similar car driven by my brother, Brian.

Leaving Salt Lake City

Day One – July 27, 2002 – I push off from Salt Lake City's Temple Square at four in the morning in Art's custom three-wheeled cycle. In six hours, I complete my fifty-three mile goal. I feel great. Why not push further? So I push an extra twenty-eight miles! My brother, Jeremy rides beside me on a bicycle. This is fun.

Day Two – There is some uphill and a twenty-eight mile per hour headwind. I have to push hard. I even have to push downhill. This is not so fun. My arms are weary, my neck and shoulders ache. I quickly gain a greater appreciation for Art Berg's four-hundred-mile record. By the end of the day, my hands are blistered and bloodied. The doctors and my wife ask me to stop, before I do permanent damage. I'm not going to reach my goal today. I did twenty-eight extra miles yesterday, so I'm still on schedule. Tomorrow will be easier.

Day Three – It isn't easier. I'm in trouble. Head winds continue. I still have to push my chair downhill. This isn't what I trained for. It is a lot harder than I thought. Mechanical failures. Two flat tires. Broken drive-chain. My back hurts. I didn't know a numb back could hurt. My hands hurt. How can my hands hurt? They're paralyzed. This is not much fun.

Day Four – Beaver Mountain. I've been dreading this. It's a

climb of twenty nine hundred feet in just four miles. I am slower than a turtle. I am on wheels, that's true, but wheels roll backward, too. This is no fun at all. Getting in Guinness doesn't seem so great now.

My father is with me. So is most of my family. Nice big motor home, remember? Support team, remember? All the comforts of home, remember? Mom brought my favorite meals, but I am now too tired to eat.

I pause in utter exhaustion. My wheelchair stops dead as soon as I quit pushing. I have to hold on to keep from rolling back. Dad is beside me in an instant.

"Dad, I can't do this. I can't. I thought I could, but I can't." I say it matter-of-factly. I don't even have the energy to whine. I am tired – beyond tired – and I still have six more days ahead – *if* I stay on schedule. "I am beat. Finished."

Dad says, "Don't think about six more days. Just do one more day. Just for me, son. Just one. If you're really done, I'll understand."

I am too tired to argue.

Day Six – I start down the other side of the mountain. Dad is right! Just keep pushing and suddenly things turn your way. Momentum will take over. Momentum is your friend. But that happy thought doesn't last long, as momentum and gravity quickly take me from zero to thirty-nine miles per hour. Thirty-nine miles per hour doesn't seem like much – unless you are only four inches off the pavement. It's pretty scary, but I make up a lot of time. Great! Maybe this *will* work. I feel better. I'll do it one day at a time, like Dad said.

We begin our trek across the Southern Utah desert. Now "one day at a time" is clearly *not* going to work. Asphalt temperatures hover at one hundred and twenty-two degrees during the day. It is one hundred and twenty at two in the afternoon. Silvery images dance off the pavement. I am pretty sure one of those is an angel on silvery wings coming to take me home.

When I decided to get in Guinness, I thought I'd be "hot stuff," but I didn't realize how hot I was really gonna get! I may be numb from my neck down, but the sound of black asphalt sizzling is unnerving.

Ever hear of Mormon crickets? They are huge – big and brown – about the size of overgrown cockroaches. Mormon crickets have a tendency to go on periodic family outings. They must have been planning this trip to coincide with mine, because coincide it did.

We are talking millions of bugs here. They move in waves – mostly crawling, some flying, like an advancing army with spotters in helicopters. They hit that stretch of highway and fry. Miles and miles, millions and millions – *billions.* Layers of dead crickets cover the highway.

I am sitting only four inches above the pavement, which is covered one inch deep with bugs. It is like pushing through pebbles – but I have to keep going. They pop and smell like burning popcorn!

Why did I choose to attempt this marathon in July? Because it is easier for a quadriplegic to cool off than it is to warm up. Ice and a wet towel will do it.

But this is too much. There is an executive council meeting in the air-conditioned motor home. We decide I should start working the night shift. Now I wait until eleven p.m. to allow the day – and the asphalt – to cool.

"One day at a time" becomes "one night at a time." I push off in the dark, heading toward the light reflected in the sky from the Vegas strip. That heavenly glow becomes my guide. Even from eighty-one miles away, the lights brighten the night sky. It is lovely, but honestly, I am torn up, broken up.

I push two hours on the ninth day. Then everything stops working. My body gives up. Remember, as one who deals with quadriplegia, I don't have any body strength. I have my neck and shoulder muscles and my biceps. That's it. It's like the Vikings trying to push a dragon ship through high seas with the cook and cabin boy at the oars and everyone else asleep in the hold.

The extra miles my ego pushed in the beginning have zapped me and no motivational mantra of, "One day at a time – or one night at a time," is going to get me into Guinness. My wife and my dad offer encouraging words.

"Honey," Shondell says, "how about trying just one *hour*

tomorrow? If you can't make it, we can go home." Now it's "one hour at a time"? Whatever happened to "one day at a time?"

Shondell gets me up at six the next morning to try again. She is happy and excited. I am not. She dresses me. I let her. I must conserve every ounce of energy I can.

I push.

One hour.

I collapse.

Instead of counting one day at a time, or even one hour at a time, I am now down to counting mile markers. Reduce big strides into small steps – and keep on going.

But can I really do this? Even one *mile* at a time? I have gone past three mile markers and the next one is nowhere in sight. How do I do ninety more miles? I can't even do one more. I *can't* do this. I am too tired to weep. After four hundred and forty-one miles, a measly ninety miles is going to stop me. Stop me from what? Breaking the world record? No. I beat the world record forty miles ago. This is *my* goal, not anyone else's, and it is tearing me apart that I can't get *DOne* what I set out to do.

My wife doesn't say anything. Dad steps in, "Son, don't give up. Break down the goal even more. Instead of mile markers, count the yellow stripes in the middle of the road. They come faster. See if that helps."

The next day, I count stripes. It actually works. I do seven hundred and twenty eight stripes that day.

Every time I felt like giving up on this journey through the desert, I would break my goal into smaller increments – one day at a time, one hour at a time, one mile at a time – and now one yellow stripe at a time. In order to survive and succeed, I have to focus on the simple task at hand and do it. Keep the goal in mind, yes; but keep my eye on the task at hand. It kept me going when I was under a bale of hay – breathe, breathe, breathe. It worked then, and it seems to be working now. Maybe I *can* do this.

Tonight, I sleep the sleep of the Pharaohs – for fourteen long, blissful hours. It is time for one last try. Mind the task at hand. Keep my mind on the goal. Try and try again.

I am pushing uphill. I can't even *see* my goal, Las Vegas – the Jewel of the Desert – beckoning the weary traveler with soft hotel beds, swimming pools... All I see is a long, black, hot highway, decorated with yellow stripes, stretching into the distance – uphill.

If I just count the stripes, maybe, maybe, maybe... seven hundred fifty eight – seven hundred fifty nine – seven hundred sixty...

Finally, I see the lone, lonely mile marker. I am out of breath. I can't even groan. *Seventeen miles to go.* This is impossible. I have nothing left – nothing. This time, I really don't. I am beyond done. No motivational mantra will move me one more marker.

I reach down into my soul and push painfully. One last push. Personal torture has now become a way of life. I just want to get past stripe number two thousand seven hundred and sixty-three. Suddenly my bike starts rolling on its own.

Wait! Stop it! Don't push! No one can push. That's not allowed. I look behind me numbly. Who is pushing me? No one? An angel?

Nope. I have crested the hill. *It is all downhill from here – all seventeen remaining miles!*

I never thought about that. After going literally as far as I could go, dividing and sub-diving my goal into smaller and smaller steps until there is nothing left – *in me* – Providence steps in. Aching shoulders, blistered and bandaged hands, don't matter

Chad entering Las Vegas

anymore. Providence is pushing me to get in Guinness.

I coast into Las Vegas on three wheels and a prayer.

They shut down all stoplights on the strip. Providence keeps pushing. At nine thirty in the morning, with traffic signals stopped and a motorcycle police escort, I coast my way to the Mirage Hotel and Casino. After eleven days, I cross the finish line. It is exactly ten years to the day that Art Berg completed his marathon.

A cheer goes up from thousands of people I have never met. I weep and grin as I realize the value of the lesson just handed me. It's not just about support – with which I was blessed in abundance. It's not just about preparation and planning – which is important. It's not just counting breaths to survive, counting stripes to progress, and doing the small things to get the big thing *DOne*. It's more than that.

When you decide what you are going to do, and give all you've got – really give it all – right down to the soles of your numb and blistered feet – you may get a push from Providence and get all you desire.

You may even get into Guinness.

"In life, unlike chess,
the game continues after check mate."

~ Sir Isaac Asimov

Seventeen

A Family Complete

In Shondell's words

Christian takes after his father. He's a tease. When he helps his dad put his shoes on, he still thinks its fun to put them on the wrong feet. He is now taller than his parents and protective of both of us. He loves to work outside, taking care of the animals. This young man is amazingly capable and responsible – he literally runs our ranch. He works as hard as any man. In that respect, he truly is his father's son. His finest quality is that he's sensitive and big-hearted. He wants to make people

Christian gets his Eagle

feel better. If an animal gets hurt on the ranch, it really affects him. In that respect he is my son.

Kyler playing soccer

Our second son, Kyler is the one who took his first steps the day Chad took his last. Kyler is a mischievous little fireball – our very own Dennis the Menace. He's always been an avid sports fan. As early as age four, he would choose to watch a major league baseball game over cartoons. If I would play soccer with him eight hours a day, he'd be in heaven. The best way to get Kyler to do a job is to turn it into a game, preferably one that imitates soccer.

We love our family. Chad worked hard to reclaim his life. That included reclaiming his role as husband, father and provider. He has done that in ways that exceed everyone's expectations, including his own. His willingness to change made the difference. By modifying the way he interacted with me and his boys after his accident, he created a better relationship than ever before.

Even in his condition, or perhaps because of the increased determination and focus spawned by his condition, Chad begins to meet and exceed our financial goals. As he recovers his ability to provide for his family, dreams we once thought gone return. We decide to sweeten our family recipe by adding a daughter to our family of boys.

When we were first married, we talked of adopting a handicapped child from Thailand. In his letters from Thailand, Chad described walking down the streets of Bangkok and seeing hundreds of children begging for handouts. Every one of them, it seemed, had a physical deformity of some kind. Chad said that in Thailand and many other countries where families struggle desperately for survival, it was not uncommon for parents to purposely injure their infant children. They might cut off a hand or an arm – something visible that would attract attention and sympathy. The parents would then send their intentionally handicapped children to the streets to beg for money from generous tourists. I could hardly believe that any parent could do this to their child, but Chad sadly assured me it is true.

He told me that if the government proves the parents to be responsible for intentionally injuring their children, they send them to prison and place the children in a state run orphanage. These orphanages are a favorite of the missionaries. Every week, usually on their day off, they spend time there.

Ranging in age from two to ten, these beautiful children with big dark eyes and amazing smiles greeted Chad and his companions with delight. Chad listened to their adventures and read stories to them in their own language. He would get down on his hands and knees and let the children jump on his back and go for "horsey rides."

The children would laugh and shriek gleefully and have a wonderful time. They loved the fact that someone would spend time with them, listen to them and let them know how important and loved they are. This is my Chad – still today.

As I read the accounts of his interaction with these special children, I realized that Chad would be a wonderful father. It's one of the reasons I wanted a large family.

One boy in particular, Frankie, really touched Chad's heart. Frankie was about eight years old. He suffered a dislocated shoulder. Because there were no funds for corrective surgery it became a permanent disability. Every time Chad walked through the door, Frankie would run and jump into his arms and show Chad pictures he'd drawn. You could tell by the way Chad wrote about him that he truly loved that child.

Chad seemed naturally inclined to look beyond the physical challenges of these children. He could always see the bright and indomitable spirit within.

His experience with these children led us to decide that one day we'd adopt a handicapped child. After his accident, though, Chad and I agreed that one handicapped child in our home was probably enough.

We don't give up our dream of adoption, though. Once Chad establishes his speaking career, we enlist the aid of an adoption agency. Children's House International helps us fulfill our dream. After speaking with one of their representatives, we decide to look for a child from Guatemala – partly because they told us that adoptions were going well in that country. They provide us with pictures and medical information about the children available for adoption.

When we see the pictures of Gracee Jo, we know this little angel was sent to earth on July 27, 2004, just for us. We send in the necessary paperwork. We wait expectantly for the call that will tell us the processing is complete. Shortly after Thanksgiving, we get the okay to fly to Guatemala and pick up little Gracee. I am so excited to see our little girl, I can hardly sleep.

Chad wants to go with me, but since we won't know the exact date in advance, it would be difficult for him to change his speaking schedule. He decides to stay home with our boys. My sister Jennilyn, and family friends, Randy and Claudia, fly with me to Guatemala to pick up baby Gracee.

When the foster mother brings Gracee to our motel room, we can tell that she has been well tended and loved. I'd been sending care packages to make sure she had what she needed. She looked adorable in one of the little outfits I had sent. As I signed the final papers, Gracee's foster mother rocked her to sleep. She laid her on the bed, kissed her gently, and quietly left.

I realize she is going away empty-handed, knowing she will probably never see this child again. I hope she knows that she has made a wonderful difference, not only in the life of this orphan, but in the lives of her new family.

Gracee arrives at the airport, met by "her boys"

Waving pink and white balloons, family and friends greet us at the Salt Lake International Airport. They gather around, cooing and making those silly noises mature adults make when a wee child grabs their hearts. Everyone wants to hold Gracee, especially Christian and Kyler. The boys approve of their new baby sister. They are especially happy, because they can go off with Chad and not feel bad about leaving their mother all alone.

"Now she can play with the baby," Kyler says.

And I do.

Two years later, we take in a nine-year-old boy who also needs a family. Now, we have another son. Jordan has had a hard life and missed a lot of school, due to circumstances beyond his control. He has faced challenges that most adults never experience. During the first nine months he was with us, Jordan endured three major surgeries to repair a severe cleft pallet.

At first, because of the extreme challenges in his early life, school is a struggle for Jordan. He isn't up to par socially, and his grades suffer. Now he is involved in soccer, basketball, and scouting and usually brings home good grades. We are incredibly proud of this young man. He has many friends and is a major part of our family. He is a wonderful big brother, supportive of his new brothers and devoted to his baby sister.

Christian and Kyler – and now Jordan and Gracee. Our family is complete – for now. But are we *DOne?* Who knows what tomorrow will bring?

Jordan receiving his Arrow of Light as a Scout

Out of the mouths of babes...

~ Matthew 21:16 KJV

Eighteen

State Fair

I have a great executive team. Machiavelli said if you want to be a great leader, you must gather around the best people, for they will reflect on you *and you will learn from them.* 6 My executive team is my family: Christian, Kyler, Gracee, Jordan, Shondell, the CMO (Chief Mommy Officer), as well as other family, friends and employees who work with me.

I have traveled throughout North and South America, Europe, Australia, Africa, Canada, and New Zealand, helping companies, associations and individuals get things done. I speak about focused leadership, recognizing and acting on opportunity in change; developing efficient, effective and safe work habits; and appreciating the value of diversity in getting the job *DOne.*

I thought I was pretty knowledgeable in all of the above.

Well, it appears I have more to learn.

It is family day. The six of us pack up and head for the fairgrounds. The State Fair attracts folks from all around, including many local homeless – and those passing for homeless – looking for a handout.

They stake out strategic locations at the entrance and exit of the fairgrounds. From there, they catch the attention – and hopefully the sympathies – of the crowd with their cardboard signs.

Some are designed to tug at your heart:

"Homeless and pregnant, please help."

"Veteran. Need medicine."

---

6 Prince and Other Writings by Niccoló Machiavelli

"Anything is a Blessing."

Some are clever and funny:

"Need cash for alcohol research."

"I'll bet you $1 you'll read this sign."

And my favorite:

"Obama isn't the only one who want's change."

Each of them has some kind of container – usually a used plastic soda cup or a tin can – into which passersby can drop their contributions. Most are dressed shabbily. Some have shopping carts loaded with all their earthly possessions.

I think to myself "Why would anyone burden themselves by dragging around all their junk?"

I do not realize, at the time, that I may well be doing the same thing.

A couple of them are playing instruments – one, a harmonica, another, a flute.

As we enter the fair, we pass close by one of them. My family does, that is. I keep my distance. I push my wheelchair forward, studying the pavement carefully to avoid eye contact.

"Come on," I mumble, trying to keep my family moving and avoid interaction with these people. I move ahead. The leader in these situations must move forward, thereby inspiring his team to pick up the pace, right?

My son, Jordan picks up his pace, too, but apparently, he didn't get the memo. He catches up to me and asks, "Dad, can I have five dollars?"

I push my chair faster, ignoring my son's request.

Jordan repeats, "Dad, can I have five dollars?" Again, my response is to not respond.

Once we get past these homeless folk, I stop to talk with Jordan. Using my senior executive wisdom, I will help him understand a bit more about life. "Son, these people just sit around all day asking people for money. That's what they do for a living."

Jordan retorts, "Dad, don't *you* just sit in your chair all day long and make a living? Dad, you owe me five bucks, remember, for good grades. Can I please have my five dollars now?"

I give in. This boy is going to head up my marketing team in a few years. I am sure of it. "Okay, Jordan. Here's your five bucks."

I count out five ones, because I know he wants to give a dollar to the man we passed.

Jordan runs back and puts it in the man's tin cup. Not just a dollar – the entire five bucks!

Before I can impart more wisdom to Jordan, Christian politely says, "Dad, you owe me five bucks, too. May I please have it?"

My protest is slight and my somewhat shorter lecture is listened to, and equally ignored.

Shondell is not saying a word.

Reluctantly, I give Christian the five dollars I owe him – five one-dollar bills so he can give one or two to the homeless fellow. Surely, Christian won't give all his worldly wealth to the poor. I am forgetting that his name is actually "Christian."

Christian follows Jordan's example. He walks over and gives the homeless fellow all five bills. The man, grateful for his good fortune, stops playing his harmonica long enough to voice a humble, "Thank you."

Ten-year-old Kyler follows suit. He is owed five bucks, too. Of course he is. I sigh deeply, pull a five-dollar bill from my wallet and give it to him. I have no more ones – but what does it matter – they aren't listening to me. Shondell is not helping. In fact, she seems to be enjoying this entire fiasco.

Smiling from ear to ear, Kyler gives the man his five-dollar bill.

My sweet little Gracee, seeing what her big brothers are doing, tugs on my sleeve, "Dad, my room is clean. Can I have five dollars, too?"

I am a beaten man. Still no help from Shondell and there is nothing left of me. No pride at all, just a quickly deflating wallet. Without a word, I take out another five-dollar bill and put it into my daughter's hand.

Short-lived in her tiny grasp, it goes right into the man's cup. In less than fifteen minutes, this man has acquired twenty bucks from our little company. He is now a professional musician in a whole other tax bracket, thanks to the generosity and kindness of my children and their willingness to muscle past my prejudice.

It is a wonderful family day. We wander freely about the fairgrounds. We follow the crowds through the farm exhibits, check out the blue ribbon lambs and pigs, and pet the sheep and baby goats.

We play the games, winning nothing but a good time. We ride the rides, consume hot dogs and fizzy soda and get pink cotton candy sticky-ness all over everything.

It is a great time, but my mind keeps wandering back to the harmonica man and his apparently destitute comrades, each holding down their own little corner at the gates to the fair like the beggar, Lazarus, at the rich man's gates.

As slowly as the illumination of the rising sun lights the world before the dawn, I get it. It dawns on me that the things that I am teaching and preaching to others are now being taught to me by my executive team. Some of these folks may be conning us, but who are we to judge?

What about the man who seems down on his luck and is playing a harmonica or flute to entertain the crowds in hopes of gaining financial support? He is doing something. He is entertaining us. Who am I to judge him?

I am fairly certain that some people judge me. How many, do you suppose, glance sideways at my emaciated body slumped in a wheelchair and assume I am a drain on society? Perhaps they look on me with pity. Maybe they feel that the world would be better off without people like me.

It is a sobering thought.

As we leave the fair that evening, we see the same gentleman, sitting in the same spot, playing the same tune on his harmonica. It has been a long day. He is still at work getting the job done. My executive team looks at me. I am way ahead of them. Even a CEO can learn!

I say, "Why don't we get him something to eat before we leave?"

There's a Burger King across the way. I pull out a twenty dollar bill and tell the boys to go get him a hamburger and shake and bring back my change.

Of course, there is no change. They spend it all. They bring back enough food to last the man a week.

We drive home in silence. The kids are asleep in the back of the van. Shondell sits quietly beside me with a funny little smile on her face. I am not saying anything, either. What a difference a day makes – especially when you have an executive team like mine.

By the way, I misspoke. I said there was no change. In fact, there was change – in me.

Doing things differently starts with seeing things differently – challenging our perceptions and re-examining our assumptions. My team helps me do that every day – especially my kids. My team *ROCKS*!

Hope is a waking dream.

~ Aristotle

Nineteen

The Man in the Red Cape

Life isn't fair, it just is – *fairly wonderful!*

Many people contributed to the "fairly wonderful" life I enjoy today; emergency medical teams, doctors, rehab professionals, family, friends…

This chapter celebrates the legacy of my friends, Christopher Reeve and Art Berg. Their determination and perseverance in the face of overwhelming challenges inspire and encourage me every day. Art Berg knew me personally, Christopher Reeve did not, but I consider them both mentors and friends.

I have read and reread their books many times, *The Impossible Just Takes A Little Longer* by Art Berg, and *Still Me* by Christopher Reeve help me along the incredibly difficult path of an increasingly wonderful journey. This amazing journey seemed impossible ten years ago, as I lay on a hospital bed fighting for my life.

Christopher Reeve, Art Berg and I share many similarities, personally and professionally. It is my hope that this book, *Doing What Must Be DOne,* inspires others to move beyond their perceived limitations into a rich and rewarding life just as the writings of Chris and Art inspired me to survive and prosper.

Christopher Reeve was amazing, not just because he accomplished so much, but because he did it with an attitude of compassion. To help you better understand his amazing success in overcoming his profound disabilities, think about my paralysis as I have described it. Then think about this: I was much better off than Chris.

If I'd broken my neck just one inch higher, I'd have been unable to breathe, unable to shift or move a muscle from my neck down, just like Chris. In fact, if my injuries had been as extensive as Chris's, I would not have survived long enough for my wife to reach me, much less the emergency team.

Before his accident, Christopher Reeve was a consummate water sports enthusiast. He loved swimming, sailing, scuba diving, skiing. He was also an accomplished horseman. It was, in fact, while riding in an equestrian event that he had his near-fatal accident that left him completely paralyzed from the neck down.

The world was shocked. Christopher Reeve was an accomplished actor, happily married, a real life "superman" admired by millions. He had a wonderful life and many dreams yet to fulfill. The world assumed Superman was done for. Superman proved them wrong.

The other "Superman" in my life, Art Berg, also had many wonderful dreams at the time of his accident. He was driving with a friend to Utah to finalize marriage plans with his beautiful fiancé, Dallas. His car went off the road in the dead of night. Art was thrown headfirst from the vehicle, his neck was broken and he was instantly paralyzed. As he lay in the dark unable to move, he wondered if his dreams were over. They weren't.

Both Christopher and Art were headed for a fairly wonderful life.

When you become paralyzed, the level of injury at which you are initially classified is extremely important. Christopher Reeve was a C1-C2 meaning that he had broken the top two cervical vertebrae. He had no feeling or movement from his neck down.

Art's C6 vertebra was broken. Art had his shoulders, some chest muscles, a working diaphragm, and could speak, albeit only a whisper at first.

My C3, C4 and C5 were fractured.

Though all three of us were classified as quadriplegic, Art and I were better able to survive the initial trauma than was Chris. We could breathe on our own, at least well enough to survive until we were found and emergency medical help could be called.

Chris was fortunate, because friends were instantly at his side and emergency medical help immediately available. Otherwise, he would not have survived more than a few minutes.

The location of the break is not only significant in our chance of immediate survival, but the severity and location of the injury also dictates what we lost and what we have left. It forecasts what we can and cannot do, now and in the future, according to medical science. Of course, with perseverance and persistence, innovation and invention, we all ended up doing more than medical science said was possible – so I use the term "dictates" advisedly.

This is an important part of the meaning and message of our experiences. Even though well-meaning friends and expert counsel may tell you something is impossible, please take my word for it, "impossible" is only an estimate. Whether an injury or paralysis is physical, mental, emotional or financial, there is power inside each of us – and a Power outside us – that can move us beyond our assumed or predicted limitations.

Art and Chris have passed on. I feel they watch over me. From time to time, I seem to hear them whisper, "You can do a little more."

I continue to improve many years after I was supposed to have reached my "improvement plateau." Do my abilities actually improve – or just my ability to figure out how to do things differently? I don't know for sure. I do believe they are with me, helping me advance one small step at a time, beyond medical predictions.

One thing Chris, Art and I shared in the beginning was difficulty in breathing. We required respirators in order to survive our first weeks or months. It took Christopher Reeve more than a year before he could breathe on his own.

He spent thirty days in a hospital immediately following his accident. Because of the nature of his injuries, the fact that he survived at all was considered a miracle. He had to be resuscitated more than once. He developed pneumonia and a urinary-tract infection, ulcers and skin lesions. When he finally realized the significance of his injury, he considered suicide. He told his wife, Dana, that it might be better for everyone if he died.

When he said that, she cried. Then, drying her tears, she said gently, "I will support whatever you want to do, because this is your life and your decision. I want you to know that I'll be with you for the long haul, no matter what."

Dana then added the words that Chris insisted saved his life, "You're still you – and I love you." Those profound words inspired the title of his book *Still Me,* a wonderful inspirational read, which I highly recommend.7

Dana encouraged Chris to give it two years. "[Then] if life is too agonizing, let's re-evaluate." Perhaps she believed – or hoped, which is sometimes more powerful than believing   that no medical diagnosis could limit her husband's indomitable spirit. Later, Chris said that if he hadn't felt that her belief and support was real, he likely would have given up. Dallas and Shondell supported Art and I the same way. Their belief in their sweethearts, even when we despaired, is the real meaning of "the power behind the throne."

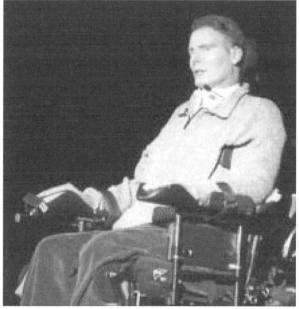

Christopher Reeve, 1995

In his book, *Still Me,* Reeve wrote about the first *Superman* movie and the interviews he gave to promote it. He was asked

---

7 Still Me: Christopher Reeve, New York, Random House, 1998

repeatedly, "What is a hero?" He would respond without much thought. "A hero is someone who commits a courageous act, without considering the consequences."

After his injury, Reeve changed his definition. He said that a hero was "an ordinary individual who finds the strength to persevere and endure in spite of overwhelming obstacles." Reeve is right. Ordinary people who overcome personal tragedies are heroes – particularly when they help or inspire others. There are countless unsung heroes who experience tragedy in their lives and find ways to go on. They do so not only for themselves, but for their families, friends, and employees who look to them for leadership or simply love them and whose lives would be lessened by their loss.

Christopher Reeve used the power of his Superman image and his celebrity status to bring hope to others facing difficult or painful circumstances. He pushed for increased work in the area of spinal cord injury. Medical scientists tend to look at spinal-cord injuries as hopeless. Research in this field was considered a dead-end street, the graveyard of neurobiology. Reeve refused to accept this. He advocated that doctors remove the word *hopeless* from their vocabulary. He understood the negative impact of the word, having been told his desire to regain any mobility was hopeless.

Reeve refused to accept this diagnosis and, when he recovered sufficiently, began speaking out. He insisted that medical professionals change their attitudes and the way they speak to those suffering spinal cord and other catastrophic injury. "Research should not be reckless, but it does need to be fearless." 8

Superman did get resistance. Many in the medical profession felt that Reeve was giving false hope. They felt patients needed to face the "reality" of their circumstances and get on with their lives from that "realistic" perspective. Our super hero pushed back with something that could withstand the withering power of kryptonite. The power of hope. Some called it false hope, but I believe, as Chris did, that there is no such thing as false hope. And, even if there is,

---

8 Jerome Groopman – interview for The New Yorker magazine

which would be worse, false hope or false hopelessness?

I understand why medical professionals wish to be "real" with their patients. I do. But what is reality? Do we really know how high the human spirit can rise when it spreads the wings of hope? Hopelessness is deadly kryptonite. It saps your strength. It leaves you weak and helpless.

Hope is the antidote for hopelessness. Hope is the power of Christopher Reeve, our real-life Superman. His message was clear, "Once you choose hope, anything's possible."

I, too, have gained power from hope. Many times, I dream that I am walking on a beach with Shondell. I see us strolling side by side on a Hawaiian beach where she once struggled to push my wheelchair through resistant sand.

I have been accused of being unrealistic. I am complimented by that accusation. I have seen the power of hope turn dreams into goals and transform goals into reality. I am not unrealistic. I just choose a different reality – the reality of hope. I hold that dream of walking on the beach with my sweetheart in a sacred place in my heart. I let that vision work its magic, making more meaningful the simple things I do every day – things I was never supposed to be able to do. These simple things have empowered me to travel the world and make a real difference in the lives of others. Perhaps someday these simple things will allow me to walk on that beach with my sweetheart.

Christopher Reeve also had a similarly inspiring dream. He loved water sports and had been a lifelong sailor. In his dream, he is sailing in the moonlight, the spray off the bow dampening his face and hair. One afternoon, he woke up and his hair *was* wet. A nurse was giving him a shampoo. He was wrenched back into the reality of pain and paralysis – but he held on to the magical power of his dream.

Chris's dream empowered him to move beyond the "plateau of improvement." The plateau of improvement is that point in time when a patient reaches the highest level of improvement possible, medically speaking. Most medical professionals establish it to be one year after a paralyzing incident.

It is more than a year – significantly beyond the "plateau of improvement" – before Chris learns to breathe on his own. But he does. He continues to improve in other unexpected ways. His improvements may have come in small increments, but they gave him great results. Once he could breathe he could move. He could maneuver his chair backwards, forwards, left, right, fast or slow – by breathing in and out of a tube. Learning to breath gave him freedom and mobility.

Art also advanced beyond that "plateau of improvement." Contrary to medical predictions, he eventually learned to transfer himself from his wheelchair to his van and, because he regained the use of his triceps in one arm, he could even lift his wheelchair into the back. He was free to go wherever he wanted to go.

All three of us improved beyond our so-called plateau of improvement, ultimately achieving a level of function far above what was predicted.

There is one important area in which Chris differed from Art and I. I have always had a strong belief in God. Faith and prayer are as natural to me as breathing and have gotten me through some rough times. It was the same for Art. In fact, his faith reinforced my own during those extremely difficult first months.

At the time of his accident, Chris didn't consider himself a religious person. He wasn't affiliated with any formal religion and didn't have what he considered a working relationship with God. He decided, however, that if he was going to get through this incredible challenge, he needed to develop that relationship. Combined with his naturally positive attitude, that faith got him through extremely difficult times. Following his accident, he would often say, "To believe in something greater than ourselves is enough." Indeed, it is.

Perhaps the greatest time of despondency and despair for Chris was when an MRI showed that he was not a "C-2 incomplete" as he had been told. Being a C-2 incomplete meant that there was some possibility of regeneration and recovery of function below his neck. He was now informed that he was definitely a C-2 complete. That gave him little hope that he would ever regain any more function. Reeve also knew that he was facing muscle atrophy, loss of bone density, osteoporosis, and other side effects of spinal cord injury. Despair again rears its ugly head.

When Art Berg realizes the extent of his paralysis, and hears the prognosis of the medical experts, he too experiences a torrent of deeply negative thoughts. Like Christopher Reeve and me, Art despairs at what appears to be a dim future – or no future at all. His spirits spiral downward. In their sincere desire to not give him a false sense of hope, his medical advisors give Art a false sense of hopelessness.

How do you deal with hopelessness?

Hope.

Combat loss of hope with new hope. Combat loss of meaning and direction with new meaning and a new sense of direction. I said "sense of direction," because you don't necessarily have to go in a new direction. You don't have to give up on old dreams; just consider new ways of doing old things. This happened to the three of us and, I daresay, many others who get through the first and second and third wave of despair without drowning.

We didn't regain our sense of direction and meaning on our own. I am not sure we could have. We were busy focusing on how unfair things were for us and those we love. Then we discovered that, though life isn't fair, it still can be fairly wonderful!

How could we reach the conclusion that life can be "fairly wonderful" in our condition? Faith and prayer and hope and determination and stubbornness, yes, but most of all the love and support of family and friends. That is the best rehab one could ever hope for.

Never underestimate the power of friendship or family support. It is critically important to support those going through difficult times – even if your support is simply being available on the other end of a telephone line or holding someone's hand. Even if you think they can't feel it, *they will feel you.*

Chris said that the toughest part of our ordeal is how it affects everyone around us, not just us. "It is not just my injury" he said, "It is 'our injury.'"

Such experiences as we went through affect everyone around us who cares, and it is you who care, who help heal the injury or lessen its negative impact. You enhance the gift of our injury as we work through our rehabilitation and regeneration.

Chris knew he had to find a different way to be productive and not a burden. This is when he began to do that extensive groundwork regarding the importance of research to help people with paralysis. He evolved from actor to activist. "Active" is the operational word. He traveled around the country, giving speeches and bringing awareness to politicians, professors, medical personnel, and the public. He spoke to anyone who would listen. He visited rehab centers. He talked with scientists in their laboratories about the progress they were making in their research.

He also worked hard to get the 'cap' on insurance increased from one million dollars to ten million dollars for people in wheelchairs. The equipment necessary to keep nerves stimulated is expensive, yet so vital. Few people can afford it, with benefits being capped at one million dollars.

Now, lest you think that he was doing this just because he now was affected by unfortunate circumstances, please know that our superhero's charitable attitude and actions began long before his accident. He had, for example, been involved in the Make a Wish Foundation, granting wishes to dying children who wanted to meet Superman.

He had been honored before as an actor representing the fictional Superman. Now, after his accident, he was being honored as a real human being for being a real superman – a role that had real meaning for everyone in every condition and walk of life. That meant a lot to him. Chris did not want to be immortalized as Clark Kent, a fictitious Superman in movies and entertainment for everyone. He wanted to be recognized as Christopher Reeve, a real superman to the disabled and an inspiration to everyone.

He felt blessed that even after his accident, he wasn't forced to give up his beloved core profession – acting. Many who experience our level of paralysis and disability never again work in their chosen field. But Chris found another way to do what that he had always done. He enhanced his profession by becoming an accomplished screenwriter and director.

Working, serving, earning, and contributing, he became more successful as a paralytic in a wheelchair than he had ever been as an able-bodied superhero in a red cape. It was said, "He was more successful after his paralyzing accident than he had ever been before." Superman's fictional power to leap tall buildings with a single bound became real after he was paralyzed. He discovered, as my father taught me, and Art proved to me, that we can do anything we want to do, anything we ever did before, as well as or better than we ever did it – *as long as we are willing to do it differently.*

Have you ever felt paralyzed? Not necessarily physically, but perhaps emotionally or financially? Are you willing to question your perspectives and perceptions? Are you willing to consider doing things differently? Challenge what you are told you cannot do. *DO* what needs to be *DOne.* You will go faster, stronger – and even higher. You may even fly like Superman – or as I did one incredible spring day…

Who needs legs, when you have wings!

~ Chad Hymas

Twenty

Flying High

"Look Dad, you're flying!"

Those wonderful words spoken by my three-year-old son, Christian, while I struggled to regain my balance, inspired the theme of my speaking business: "Who needs legs, when you have wings?"

Flights of fancy, I believe, are as important as real flight. Of course I will never really fly. That is impossible.

Or is it?

It is a beautiful misty morning in the spring of 2003. I am driving alone on Interstate 15 near what we call The Point of the Mountain. There, the Wasatch Mountains intrude into the valley with an enormous steep ridge or "point." Winds that hit this ridge produce huge updrafts that support swooping, climbing, and diving hang-gliders. On a good day, over a dozen kites move in and out in an eclectic pattern like a free form dance of brightly colored butterflies.

Looking closely, I see the people suspended from the hang-gliders. I can't see their expressions, but can imagine their look of freedom.

I noticed them before, as I drove past this particular spot on my way to and from my ranch and the airport. This time, something new catches my eye. I pull over and watch fascinated as two people, connected in tandem, sail on the wind suspended beneath large purple and red striped wings.

This is it! This is for me! I can do this!

I exit at Draper, just north of The Point of the Mountain and locate the office of Cloud 9. The owners tell me they have taken paraplegics up and assure me there is no reason why a quadriplegic couldn't enjoy the same experience. They have to make additional arrangements to accommodate my disability, but they are happy to do it. I set up a date for the following week.

Why wait?

What happens when a procrastinator has a great idea? Nothing!9 *Action and procrastination cannot exist in the same space.* If I'm going to get something *DOne*, I better just *DO* it, right?

I am excited. I am finally going to fly – really fly! Who needs legs, when you have wings! I can do anything, if I am willing to do it differently.

They put me through a one-and-a-half hour training course, where they show me all the things to do to control a hang-glider. They show me how to twist, turn, and shift my weight to catch the draft as one catches a wave in the surf. They tell me the most important thing is to let go and have fun. This good instruction does me no good. There is no way I can do the things they advise, except the "have fun" part. *That* I can do.

Three men strap me into something resembling a sleeping bag. I prefer to call it a sleeping bag, rather than a body bag! I am strapped to the flight instructor's body above and slightly to one side, so I can catch the scenery. In addition, I must be out of the way so Chris, the instructor, can have his feet available to control the landing when we return to earth.

How ironic. Chris (my son) inspires me to fly, Chris (Superman) convinces me it's possible, and Chris (the instructor) gets the job *DOne.*

Here we go…

Ever jump to your death? Of course, you haven't. Your sense of self-preservation won't let you – unless of course you are piloting a hang glider – then, overcoming your natural fear and jumping into the void is essential to getting airborne.

A lot like life.

---

9 "Do you know what happens when you give a procrastinator a good idea? Nothing." ~ Donald Gardner

Pushing off the edge of the cliff, my worst fears are realized. We do fall – straight down! I am scared half to death. Why? I don't know. It isn't like it would hurt. Maybe it is just that natural instinct not to dive headlong into sharp jagged rocks! If I close my eyes, it won't be happening, right? My eyes slam shut. They stay that way for about fifteen seconds as I try to compose myself enough to look death in the face. This is the dumbest thing I've ever done – next to my desert marathon – or the rollercoaster ride.

Hang-gliding

We are in free fall. The ground rushing up at us…

Then, as the speed of our fall enhances the power of the wind beneath our wings,[10] lift takes over and in one beautiful heart grabbing moment, we swoop into a two hundred and fifty-foot climb. This is incredible. Indescribable. Wonderful. I am flying!

Isn't it interesting how the fear of falling often precedes the thrill of soaring?[11]

---

10 Title of a song written in 1982 by Jeff Silbar and Larry Henley - Sung by Bette Midler and Celine Dion

11 "Sometimes the thrill of soaring has to begin with the fear of falling." ~*Crystal Lewis*

It is a smooth flight, no rips, no ripples, no air pockets. We keep to the east side, close to the mountain, across the ribbon of blue that is the I-15 freeway, and to the north is Utah Lake. Tiny boats and water skiers weave white foam tracks in the blue water.

Brightly colored toy trucks and cars maneuver for position on the tiny blue freeway – little ants busily concerning themselves with their mysterious little errands.

Those vehicles carry real people with real goals and dreams, and real problems. But from this height, it seems that I am seeing what is really important, what matters most. This overview of the valley helps me realize that, if we could see life in this same perspective – an overview from a thousand feet up – we would discover that, overall, life is good; the world is beautiful.

I begin to look at things from a different perspective. Even though I lost much because of my accident, maybe I've gained much more than I've lost. I begin to understand on a deeper level how we can do the seemingly impossible, if we are willing to do it differently. After all, here I am – flying.

We can get through the difficult, sad, even dangerous frustrations of life, if we just get above it for even a minute or two and see the big picture. If we could share God's view for just a moment, we would know that no matter how tough things seem, life is an incredible journey. Whether on foot, on wheels, or on wings, we will eventually make it through just fine.

This is a beautiful experience – on bright and beautiful wings. I want it to last forever, but after only twenty minutes, my teeth begin to chatter. Even though it is a sunny spring day, I am getting cold. Remember, I have no body thermostat to turn up to burn my morning Wheaties for fuel for warmth. I've paid for a forty-five minute ride, but I better go back, before I suffer hypothermia. I'm okay with it, though. I've been flying only twenty minutes – but what a beautiful, paradigm-shifting twenty minutes.

Chris's landing is smooth and expert. They unstrap me, get me warmed up (Chris wanted to stick me in the microwave) and help me back to my van. I sit there in reverent silence marveling at what has just happened.

Mark Twain said, "Courage is resistance to fear, mastery of fear – not absence of fear. Except a creature be part coward, it is not a compliment to say it is brave!" Was I brave or crazy to try this? A little of both, I suppose – not a bad combination, if you want to gain a new perspective and a new attitude and altitude in life.

When Shondell sees the video of my flight she has a few words of "advice" for me. I promise not to do it again.

I still dream of flying, though – so I do as many things as I can to fly in as many different ways as I can to make that dream be true. Isn't it amazing what we can do, and get *DOne*, if we are willing to do it differently?

My son is right – I can fly.

Who needs legs, if you have wings?

Learn from yesterday, live for today, hope for tomorrow. The important thing is not to stop questioning.

~ Albert Einstein

Twenty-One

Corporate Paralysis

It's a bird.

It's a plane.

No. It's Super*corporation!*

How is your company doing? Is it doing okay – but not really great? There doesn't seem to be anything wrong – at least, not something you can put your finger on. Your employees are well chosen, intelligent, and talented. They do a lot, but what you really need them to do doesn't seem to get done.

Things just aren't working well.

My hands don't work well, either. There's nothing wrong with them. There are no contusions, no broken bones – not even arthritis. They should work. They don't. Neither do my legs.

Why?

Loss of communication.

Nothing from my shoulders down works well. I can't run, jump or even walk as I once did.

What happened?

Loss of communication.

I am in a wheelchair because of loss of communication? Yes. When that one-ton bale of hay fell on me, it broke my neck, damaging my spinal cord. Communication between my brain and my body was compromised.

"Corporate" "corporation" "corporeal" "corpse" – all have to do with "body." When the lines of communication in a corporation are down, communication is compromised *both* ways. The head – the "head office" – can't get through to the body and the corporate body can't send adequate feedback to the head. The CEO doesn't know what's going on downstairs and the corporate body doesn't know what's going on upstairs. Everyone is in the dark. They may be doing their jobs – but they aren't getting the job done – *because they don't really know what "DOne" looks like.*

Superman

Effective communication is a two-way street. Signals must go in both directions and those lines must remain open. Loss of communication can take down anyone or any organization, no matter how viable or strong. The mighty Superman – Christopher Reeve – was felled, not by a chunk of kryptonite, but by loss of communication. When he was thrown from his horse, his helmet saved his corporeal CEO, his brain, from the impact, but his neck was broken, his body deprived of instruction, and instantly paralyzed.

When that bale of hay fell on my head, I only suffered a broken neck. The rest of me was fine; not a contusion, not an abrasion, not a bruise, but communication between the CEO (my brain) and my feet and hands (the ones who do all the work) was compromised. That is why I can't walk or run. That is why I am in a wheelchair.

As I write this, my brain must tell my arms and wrists what to do and they "get it," but nothing gets past the arms and wrists to the hands and fingers – so they do nothing. The brain must know something, right? If it didn't, this next sentence would read: "xlosniks xhg gti z vof zll booc mzn go omd go gh zic o ghdif oun c try." That should read "Now is the time for all good citizens to come to the aid of their country (the old typing exercise)."

Though my brain is able to get some information through to my body, it can't send anything back; hence, the feeling of total disconnect. No sensation of anything below shoulders. Unless I look down, it seems I have no body at all. I feel like a floating head.

My hands and fingers get nothing and send nothing. It is my eyes that make it possible for me to type. They have to look and see what is going on and report to the CEO, so the boss can get some information to my biceps and wrists and rely on them to do the job that a thousand other muscles in my arms, wrists, hands and fingers should be doing.

They do the best they can. I type with paddles strapped to my wrists. This works okay. I can type fifty words per minute. For someone in my condition, that is darn good!

I am not complaining. I can and do a lot with my life, but I could do so much more if my brain and body could communicate better. How about you? How much more could your company do if your lines of communication were clear – both ways?

Is your body corporate communicating well with your executive team? Or is your corporeal organization suffering from a broken neck and compromised lines of communication?

You can fuddle along like I do. You can type fifty words per minute, pecking out letters with paddles strapped to your corporate wrists, and you'll do okay. But how much better would you do if your lines of communication were open and clear – in *both* directions?

You will move rapidly from "okay" to "super." That's what you'll do. Things you DO will actually get *DOne*. A paralyzed economy will cease to exist where you are concerned and you will be Super Corporation, leaping tall challenges with a single bound!

One big difference between a body corporate and my corporeal body is that *the cure for corporate paralysis is simple and easily available* – while the cure for my paralysis lies somewhere between faith healing and successful stem cell research.

Won't it be great to walk, jump and run again as you did when you were a young company? It is possible. Get those lines of communication open. Connect with your people. Invite them to communicate with you and let you know what they are feeling, thinking – what they are experiencing. Make communication a company imperative – good, honest, real communication – *in both directions*.

Your corporate "things to do list" will then become your "things that got *DOne*" list. You will enjoy such a surge of power and effectiveness that you will leap over the obstacles of any paralyzed economy and leave your competition wondering, "Is it a bird? Is it a plane? No…

…*it's* Super*corporation!"*

Do the possible in the morning.
Save the impossible for after lunch!

~ Chad Hymas

Twenty-Two

Dream Big – Think Small – Win Big

Are you where you want to be? Why not? Do you think you should have been there long ago? What is holding you back? What has you paralyzed? Do you have a magnificent goal or dream that has you intimidated into thinking it is impossible? Perhaps you feel you are not worthy of it.

What are you focused on? The enormity of the task? It's complexity? The sheer un-do-able-ness of it? The fact that no one has ever done it? Is everyone telling you that the reason no one has ever done it is because it can't be done?

I know how that feels. I do.

Be assured, however, that the big beautiful dream is not there to frustrate or intimidate you. It is there to inspire you, to energize you, to draw you to it – to *do* it and get it *DOne*.

What do you do when you are held back by doubt and despair? What do you do when you are faced with the impossible task, the insurmountable problem, the unreachable goal?

Dream Big.

Think small.

Then do it.

You will win big.

Wake up in the morning. Get up. Can you do that? If you are tired, push the "snooze button" once. Lie on your back with your eyes closed. Relax. Drift a bit. If your spouse asks what you are doing, say you are meditating. Dream about all those great big wonderful things you want to accomplish. Go ahead, dream big. Feel yourself in that sports car with the wind in your face. See yourself stepping over the threshold of your new dream home. See yourself addressing a gleeful crowd at your next stockholders meeting. Feel the excitement rise.

Now... shift your dreaming big into thinking small.

Think about what you will do today. If your spouse asks what you are doing, say you are working – because you are. Focus on six things you can do – six things you will get done today. Feel the energy pour into you.

Chad with Zig Ziglar on July 23, 2006

Get up. Follow your feet into the shower. Sing a little. How about a few lines from the theme song from Man of LaMancha? "To dream the impossible dream..." Sing it out loud – only sing it a little differently: "To dream the *possible* dream, to fight the *beatable* foe... to go where it *makes sense* to go..."

Eat a healthy breakfast and go to work. Start six minutes before you are scheduled to. Do the possible. Make six phone calls. Send six follow-up emails. Write today's affirmation to post on your blog. Write a fifty-word draft of next week's blog. Write three pages in your book. Focus on the possible in the morning. Save the impossible for after lunch!

You will succeed. Count on it. If you are overwhelmed, if the burden feels too great –breathe. Count breaths. If it seems you have too far to go, and you feel you'll never make it, count mile markers in *your* road, focusing on *your* jewel of the desert. If mile markers are too much, count the yellow median stripes – they always add up to miles and miles always add up to a successful journey.

Count pages written, phone calls made, customers served. Count floor tiles as you push slowly down your personal hall of fame. Count on your friends and your family for support. Count on yourself and count on your Creator.

Focus on the possible, the doable, and do it. Prop this book up in front of you so you can see the cover every day.

"Doing What Must Be DOne"

Remember, the root word in "doing" and "done" is "do." So, do it – every day – without fear, without faltering, and without fail. Know in your heart that when you *do* the little things, you will get the big things *DOne*.

"Healing is a matter of time, but it is sometimes also a matter of opportunity."

~ Hippocrates

The Basement

Or So I Thought

We are sent here to this planet to make a difference – I always felt it. Now I know it. We are given essential tools and talents and it is our job to make something of what we have. And what do we have?

Eyes to see; ears to hear; a brain to think; arms and hands to work; legs to get us where we are meant to go. I was born and raised in an able-bodied world – and there I would excel.

Or so I thought.

In my world, a man's worth was measured by what he could do – especially physically. A real man got up early, worked hard all day, and went to bed tired but happy, because of all he accomplished. A real man was the provider and protector. A real man was 'the man.'

That was my attitude, and it seemed to pay off. Every summer of my youth, I worked hard on my aunt and uncle's ranch; buckin' bales, driving truck, building fence. I loved hard work; besides, it kept me in shape for sports. Hard work and athletic accomplishment were signs of manhood – coming of age.

Championship trophies and business accomplishments measured our worth – taught us discipline and goal orientation. I was tough. Ambitious. My life was laid out before me, clear and straight.

Or so I thought.

I grew up and married my high school sweetheart. I honored my family traditions and values. My dad taught me to work hard. Take care of your family. Be the man. No nonsense.

I invested in an Elk ranch and built a successful landscaping business. As I had looked to my father in my younger days, two-dozen employees, and another dozen seasonal workers now looked to me for leadership. I worked as hard as my men did. I never asked anything of them that I couldn't or wouldn't do myself – or hadn't already done.

My wife, Shondell, stayed home and managed the house with order and efficiency, and raised our children. I worked from dawn to dusk, providing for them all. I was my children's protector, my lady's hero. "Me Tarzan, you Jane." That is what life is all about.

Or so I thought.

That was my world. My family needed me. They depended on me – I depended on myself. I was tough and independent. That worked, not just for me, but also for my family. That is what I believed. That was my attitude. That was the way it was.

Or so I thought.

God evidently thought differently because it changed – a bale of hay had to fall on my head to do it, but my life changed – and then, I changed. Attitudes and assumptions where challenged; belief and behavior changed; I learned a lot about who depends on who and what is really important in life.

You've read my story – or are about to. Don't stop there. Go *DO* something about something. Get something *DOne*. Make a difference. If you're already doing something about something, good for you – *you* didn't wait for a bale of hay to land on *your* head!

End of the Day...

Johnny Five

What is "healed"?

Does it mean to be restored to a former condition?

Could it also mean to get better?

If "healed" includes getting better – maybe even being better than before – could it then be that the disaster – the very situation that we are healing from – is actually an integral part of the healing process?

In the movie, *Short Circuit*, a deadly military defense robot (one of five identical robots, therefore known as "#5") is struck by lightning. The extreme voltage fries his circuits. He malfunctions – stumbles about, runs into walls – and really makes a mess of things.

In healing himself from his damaged condition, #5 rewires his own circuits and moves beyond his programming. He discovers that if something is broken, fried or melted, as much of him is, he can work around the problem and simply do it differently. He gets better – better than before. He even chooses a new name for himself "Johnny Five."

Though originally designed as a powerful and deadly killing machine – and even though he has lost none of that power (his onboard mini laser-cannon is really cool) – he becomes funny, charming, creative and kind.

Most importantly, he learns to laugh.

He evolves from a machine governed and limited by his programming and becomes "human," a living, growing, learning being, limited only by his imagination – and sense of humor.

That which initially seemed a disastrous accident, turns out to be a necessary part of the process of Johnny Five being "healed."

Johnny Five revels in being "alive." He learns that mistakes, accidents and injury – even malfunctions – are a part of life, but *life itself is not a malfunction.*

As it turns out, the bad day he was having now isn't.

Is it possible then, that the bad day you are having is an

opportunity to improve? Get better? Even heal in a way you couldn't before?

Is it possible, then, that the bad day you are having – isn't?

No, life is NOT a malfunction.

See Me As Me

Generally even well meaning people who interact with folks dealing with disabilities tend to speak to us and otherwise treat us kindly, but not as they would "normal" people.

It should be obvious that everyone has some sort of disability— many wear glasses, hearing aids or have other sensory challenges. Some are more dexterous than others. Some are graceful as Fred Astaire, while others move as if they are mired in mud. Most of us who suffer brain injury struggle with behaviors and auditory or visual misperceptions that require coping mechanisms in order to deal with simple things of life– such a making lists and leaving them prominently displayed in our special place – maybe even along with our car keys.

I strongly suggest that, in order to truly help, we have to see everyone, dealing with disabilities or not, as "normal," at least in the respect that we have the same needs and feelings and also the same worth and value as anyone else. More importantly, see us as people who can make incredible contributions when we feel we are a viable part of our group or organization.

People usually treat folks with disabilities with kindness, but not always with respect. They don't always treat us the same as they treat "normal" people. In order to truly accommodate disability, we must incorporate the individual. We must see everyone – dealing with disabilities or not – as "normal". People with disabilities not only have the same needs and feelings as anyone else, but we also have equal worth and value as anyone else.

Like anyone else, we are capable of making incredible contributions, when we feel we are a viable part of our group or organization.

The barriers most disabled people face are monumental. It shouldn't be about whether we can hold a pen or walk a straight line. For instance, when looking for a job, it should be whether we are qualified or not for the position. You don't hire a blind man to wait tables or a deaf person to answer phones; but we are employable.

My dear friend, Art Berg, was injured right before he was to be married. After he was pronounced a quadriplegic, he interviewed for jobs. While calling and trying to set up interviews, one employer was so impressed with his resume, that Art was offered the position right over the phone! However, when he arrived the next day to start, they saw he was in a wheelchair, and suddenly, a "reason" was invented why they could no longer hire him.

I was fortunate. I had no idea what I would or could do after my accident. Previously, I had owned and operated my own landscaping business. That was no longer a possibility. I had a young family to support. The future looked dismal. Soon after my accident, I spoke in church to thank our friends and neighbors for all they had done. A visitor from Las Vegas was among the congregation. When the meeting concluded, he approached me and asked if I would come and speak to his company. He even asked what my fee would be! He said he felt inspired after listening to my story and wanted his employees inspired as well. That was ten years ago.

Now, I get to travel the world, spend time with thousands of people, showing them what is possible if you believe in yourself. I have the opportunity to encourage individuals to overcome their challenges, focus on their dreams, hoping to make them become a reality.

Last year, I traveled over 300,000 miles, speaking in four countries on five continents. I have also been very blessed in my personal life. Shondell and I now have four beautiful children and live on our elk ranch. I am living the dream.

* * * * *

Do you want to know who you are?
Don't ask. Act!
Action will delineate and define you.

~Thomas Jefferson

Chad All Over the World

In the last ten years, Chad Hymas has shared his message on all 7 continents and in 38 countrics. The following pages show just a few of the many events that Chad has been priveleged to be a part of. Enjoy!

6,500 people in Nashville, TN

17,000 at Indianapolis

ACLP in Ontario, Canada

Meeting new friends at a book signing

Brothers help Chad train for his Rolling Marathon

A break during the record-setting marathon

Leaving Australia for Peru

Chad with one of Charlie's Angels, Jaclyn Smith

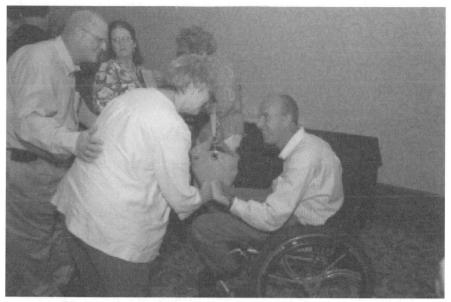

Book-signing in Europe

Bus tour in 2011

Chad designated Certified Speaking Professional, July 23, 2006

Bus Tour in Winnemucca, NV 2010

Chad with best-selling authors Phil Van Hooser and Sam Silverstein

Chad at base theater – supporting our troops

Teichert Construction, Sacramento, CA - 2006

Chad's "limo" in Bangkok

Coach Dad

Elementary school assembly

There's nothing
more important
in Chad's life
than family time.

*"No success can
compensate for
failure in the
home."
~ Bruce R.
McConkie*

FFA, 2005 in Alabama

GoYin, Hawaii - 2005

Hormel Foods, 2012 Kick-Off

Chad hunting with his three boys and friends, 2010

Hunting with Phil Van Hooser

In Germany

Chad and Shondell in Kansas City with Hall of Fame Speakers,
Dan Clark and Vince Poscente

Los Angeles, 2005

Leaders of America forum Washington, DC

In London

Love the connections!

Love their faces

Visiting a middle school in Park City, UT

*Training for the 513-mile world-record marathon
at Broken Arrow Construction*

Chad named honorary captain at Montana State homecoming

Chad speaks to a mining rescue team in Tanzania

After a speaking engagement at NASA, we got the family tour

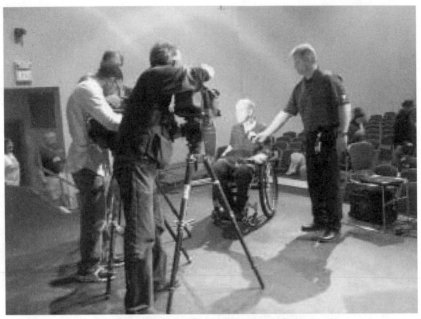

NBC Studios, post-speech

Working with student leadership at Rock Springs High School

North Ogden Junior High assembly

New Zealand, 2007

Perth, Australia

Speaking in Alaska, and then out for halibut fishing

Student body leadership council in Wyoming, 2009

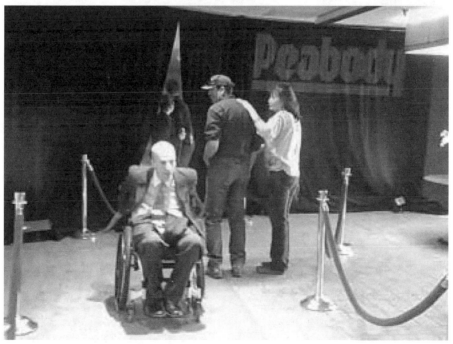

The red-carpet treatment at Peabody Energy

*Safety Health
Leadership Award,
Las Vegas*

Santiago, Chile

SOLD OUT!

Shondell surprised me with a date in San Diego

Special Olympics in St. George, UT, 2005

Spending time with our future

At a warehouse in St. Louis, 2010

Salt River Materials Group, New Mexico, 2005

Student Safety Day in Nova Scotia, 2007

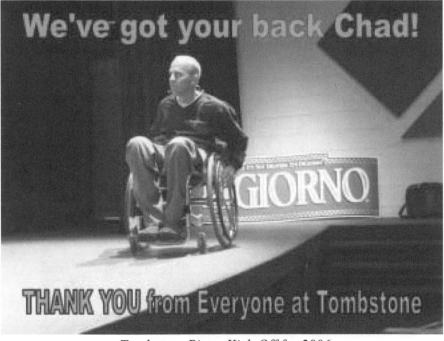

Tombstone Pizza, Kick-Off for 2006

Our tour bus, covering all 50 states

Traveling to the Arctic

Underground in Africa, 2007

United Tac, Minnesota

Speaking to Wells Fargo Bank, 2008

Westar Power Plant, 2009

With miners of Victor at their annual safety refresher

In South Africa, 2010

Chad's keynote address to23,000 people at the "Get Up" Kickoff, 2009

Chad works with kids in schools...

To think too long about doing a thing
often becomes its undoing.

~Eva Young

FOLLOW US ON:

http://www.facebook.com/chadlhymas
http://www.twitter.com/chadlhymas
http://www.linkedin.com/in/chadhymas
http://www.youtube.com/chadlhymas
http://chadhymas.com/1770/living-in-the-moment/ (blog)
http://www.chadhymas.com

To order more books, call:
1-877-BOOK CHAD

or visit:
http://chadhymasproducts.com

For bulk discounts of over 100 copies, email:
info@chadhymas.com
or call 1-435-843-5707
Fax: 435-843-5010